A Parent's Guide

Pass Your Faith To Your Children

*Through the Simple Practice of
Teaching Your Child to Pray*

Robert Bohler, Jr.

A Practical Plan For Helping Your Child
Develop Their Own Authentic Life of Faith

Pass Your Faith To Your Children

ISBN: 978-0-9915389-2-8

Cover Design: JoeSchlosser.net

Cover Photo: Unsplash.com

2021 - First Edition

PASS YOUR FAITH TO YOUR CHILDREN

"Dr. Bohler's methods for teaching children to pray have made such a positive difference in my family's daily life as Christians. It has given us special time together thanking God for our many blessings and asking God for help with challenges. The prayers I've heard from all my children (ages 13, 9, and 4) make my heart so happy and so thankful for wonderful guidance in this area. Dr. Bohler's methods are easy to understand and for any family to put into practice."

Leanna Baker

"I don't know that there's anything more important for a Christian parent to do than to cultivate their child's prayer life. It turns out to be such an easy thing to do! Just a few minutes at the end of the day, with us praying first and our child following in turn, has not only taught our children to pray but has enriched our prayer life as well. Witnessing the ease and honesty with which our children go to the Lord in prayer, from an early age, has been a rich and rewarding experience."

Matt Hoots

"We are so grateful that we had the opportunity to learn from Dr. Bohler about how to teach our children to pray. It has been such a neat experience to listen to our four children grow and develop their ability to express their thoughts, feelings, worries, and praises to God through prayer. Our children are confident in their ability to pray privately and publicly. My parents love to keep our children as often as they are able. After a weekend visit with my parents, my mother told me that she always looks forward to hearing our children pray. She said that it always makes her cry to hear how sweetly they talk to God."

Lawton and Beth Stewart

"Watching our boys mature in their relationship with God through prayer has been a tremendously rewarding experience. As toddlers, they watched us pray with them when it was time to go to sleep. As young children they learned to lead prayer before bedtime. Today, as teenagers with extremely busy schedules they stop and remind us to pray with them before they go to bed. Bedtime prayer with our boys has been a blessing in our lives by strengthening our relationship with God and each other as a family while providing our boys an eternal life lesson. Thanks, Pastor Bob."

Reuben and Robin Rudisill

"We are amid a revitalization of Christianity and the family. Dr. Robert Bohler is at the forefront of this revitalization with his teaching and writing. I have read and incorporated much of his advice into my family with rich results. The opportunity to engage Christianity under Dr. Bohler's tutelage is guaranteed to increase your faith along with that of your family."

Philip G. Gibson, Ph.D.

DEDICATION

Dedicated to my family, Kim, Robert, and John. My wife
Kim has been a wonderful companion for over 25 years. Our
two boys, Robert and John, were the ones on whom we
tested the simple practices I describe in this book. Their
lively faith continues to convince me that it is possible for
parents to pass their Christian faith along to their children.

This book is written in hopes that, because of the simple
practice I describe in this book, the church will no longer
lose its children, but raise up a new generation of disciples
of Jesus Christ.

ABOUT THE AUTHOR

Dr. Robert Bohler, Jr., known to most as Bob, is a Presbyterian pastor in the ECO denomination. He grew up in Decatur, Georgia and graduated from Georgia Tech with a degree in Industial Engineering. After working for several years in engineering, he responded to a call to ministry. He has served churches in Lakeland, Florida, Charlotte, North Carolina, and Athens, Georgia. He and his wife, Kim, have two boys. One recently graduated from the University of Georgia in Mechanical Engineering and is working as an engineer. Their youngest son is a junior at the University of Georgia. Dr. Bohler has served the church for over thirty years as a pastor. In his spare time, he plays tennis, reads theology, travels, and takes his wife to dinner.

CONTENTS

INTRODUCTION

A MEMORABLE CONVERSATION

I REMEMBER THE CONVERSATION like it was yesterday. The dear older lady in my congregation sat on the couch in front of me. As her pastor, I had gone to visit her one spring afternoon and we sat in her living room. The sky was clear, and the birds were singing; it was a beautiful day. Little did I know how this conversation would impact my life!

The woman sitting across from me was a delightful person. For many years, she had been a member of the church I was pastoring, and everyone loved her. I knew her husband before he passed away and he was a fine man, strong and quiet, but the salt of the earth.

As we talked together, she told me about her children. They were successful and had nice families. I knew them from visits at Easter and other holidays; she had reason to be proud of them. They came to see her regularly and, as grown children, took thought for her welfare. From the outside this was a set of children of which any mother would be proud.

But then she looked reflective for a moment and paused in her conversation. "There's only one thing," she said. "Three out of my four children don't go to church." "They go with me when they are here, of course, but otherwise they never go." She paused and said, "I don't understand it. We raised them right. We took them to church all the time. They had good experiences in church; at least I thought they did. What went wrong? Why don't they care about God?"

I knew that what she was saying about trying to raise her children right must have been true. Her family had been in church almost every time the doors were open. She and her husband were very involved in the church and, in that sense, were good examples for their children. As a couple, they were the salt of the earth and, like all their friends in that era, made sure they raised their four children in church. Each Sunday they would have taken them to Sunday School and worship. Vacation Bible School was a staple of their summer experience. They must have talked about God and faith at home with their children.

But apparently it did not "take." Three out of their four children had essentially rejected their parents' beliefs. Of course, they would not have said that in so many words, but their actions revealed the truth. As grown adults, these children did not go to church, because they did not think it important. Nor had they made much effort to raise their own children in the church. The faith that this wonderful lady held so dear had been essentially rejected by the majority of the children she had raised. She worried about their salvation and what she had done wrong and it was a source of great apprehension for her.

I remember that the woman looked away and I could see the moisture in her eyes. I looked away too because I didn't know what to say. At that time I did not have any children of my own so I did not have much experience in parenting. Wanting to give her some comfort, I responded, "You never know when the seeds you have planted will bear fruit. They will come back to God when the time is right." I knew that certainly *might* be true, but my heart was not in the words because there was little evidence that made me confident of such an outcome.

This dear lady and her husband had done all the right things in terms of passing their faith along to their children, or so they thought. As it turned out, however, it did not work. Now she wondered if it was too late? Unfortunately, the likelihood is that it was. She had missed her opportunity to instill faith in her children and would not get it back.

Sadly, in the years since that conversation, I have heard this story many times. Good Christian people who raised their children in the church, find that their efforts to pass on their faith did not work. They assumed that taking their children to church would be sufficient to help their children find their own faith. They assumed that experiences in Sunday School and youth group would be sufficient. They assumed that their job, as the parent, was to take their family to church and be a good person. As it turned out however, it was not enough. Something was missing. But what?

A CRISIS IN CHRISTIAN FAMILIES

The conversation with this dear lady was a number of years ago, but it has haunted me ever since, especially as I now have children of my own. When my children were born, I started to ask myself some fundamental questions. I wondered if it were possible that my children also might grow up in a Christian home but not be impacted by the faith I hold so dear. How do you pass the faith along to your children? How do you help the faith impact their heart and not just be a veneer of religion? What does it take for them to acquire real faith?

Being a pastor, this was a double concern. We all know how the "preacher's kids" turn out. They are the ones crawling under the pews during the service, downing all the grape juice from the little cups after communion is over, when they think no one is looking (I know this from experience), and generally acting like they own the church. They feel like they own the church, of course, since they are there all the time. As a pastor, I began to think and worry, about how to make sure my kids caught the faith. I also wanted to make sure they were not so inoculated by being in church all the time, that they never caught the real thing.

The problem of the dear lady is not unique. In fact, it is widespread. It is the greatest unrecognized crisis in Christian families and the church today. Christian families are losing their children at an alarming rate. A study by a reputable Christian research organization, the Barna Group, discovered some disturbing statistics. It found that, after the age of fifteen, 59% of young people will disconnect from the church and the Christian faith for an extended period of time.[i] That is almost 6 out of 10 young people. These young people, who reach an age where they no longer have to attend church with their families, gradually but steadily drop out. They drop out of church and increasingly disconnect from any real life of faith.

The hope of church leaders and parents is that they will eventually come back to the faith of their youth. The reality, however, is that many of them will not! Increasingly in today's world, they will not ever come back to the faith! Christian parents are losing their children away from the faith and it is a crisis of immense proportions. If you have not been thinking about this issue as a Christian parent, you need to start!

Most of us are aware of the problem, if we think about it. Almost everyone knows good Christian people whose grown children never darken the doors of a church. They may occasionally visit when home for a holiday. But they are not connected with the church in any significant way and show little evidence of a living faith.

What is disturbing for these families is that the parents thought they were doing all the right things. They took their children to church. They volunteered in Vacation Bible School, as ushers, and on church boards. Their children went to youth group where they were supposed to learn the faith. But something along the way did not connect their child to the heart of Christianity. The distressing problem is that for many parents, it is too late. Their children are now grown and outside the church. All they can do is hope, pray, and wonder what went wrong.

This is not just a theoretical question, but an existential one for parents. We are not just talking about statistics here or about someone else's children. This has to do with your children! That you pass Christianity along to your children is of the utmost importance. What would you give to be able to do this? The answer is that you would pay any amount and go to any length, if you thought it would guarantee your child's Christian faith and eternal salvation! But what is it you need to do?

WHY DOES THIS MATTER?

As a parent, you might ask, "Does this really matter?" You might say, "I'm going to raise my child to be a good person; that's really what they need most." It sounds great to raise your child to be a good person and it is, but it is not all your child needs. If you only raise your child to be a good person, you place them in great danger of losing their way in life because they do not have a sufficiently sturdy foundation on which to build their life.

Think about your child's life as a building. Every building has a foundation and the taller the building, the deeper and stronger the foundation needs to be. No one would imagine trying to build a tall skyscraper without laying a solid foundation, because the first significant storm that came through would create serious problems. Your child's life is like a great building that you are trying to help them build. You want it to be tall and strong. You want it to be able

6

to withstand the storms of life. Because of this, your child's life needs a foundation and one that is stronger than just being a good person. It's great to be a good person but ultimately questions arise, such as, "Why?" "Why should I be a good person?" "Why should I be honest?" "Why should I be faithful to my spouse?" "Why should I be honest when I can get ahead by bending the rules?" "Why should I think about others instead of only myself?" "Why should I do the right thing?" All these questions and many more are ones your child will wrestle with at some point in their life. Eventually they will face temptations to veer off the path of being good. Those temptations will be strong, perhaps stronger than you can imagine at this point. What is it that is going to hold them to the right path and keep them in the way of life?

The truth is, there is only one good and true motivation for an honest, decent, unselfish life; it is faith in God. Why is this? Because every other incentive can be overcome with a little self-deception, external persuasion, or just sheer laziness. Christianity gives people a moral, ethical, and spiritual foundation on which to build a life that is not easily shaken, even by the worst of storms or the most enticing temptations. A deep and real faith in God can help your child care about others, do the right things, and makes an impact beyond merely their own self-interest. Faith in God will give your child a sturdy foundation because their foundation is God, and he cannot be moved or manipulated. He does not change with the winds of culture or popular opinion. He is the one and only foundation that is strong enough for a great life. Why would you not want your child to have this foundation for their life, a foundation that enables them to both endure life's storms and stand strong as an example to others, including, one day, their own families.

Think about the lives of famous people; they are often a train wreck. How can this be possible? They have money, fame, success, and adulation. Isn't that what makes a person happy? The answer is, "No," of course; this isn't what makes people happy. It's why many celebrities are not happy; fame and fortune are all they have! They have no real core for their lives other than themselves. As most of us recognize, happiness does not come from material things; it comes from other places and primarily from having good relationships with people we love and especially God.

The problem is that happiness can be very elusive. In fact, those who chase after it don't find it. Happiness is not achieved by pursuing it but as a result of having other goals to pursue that give one a higher purpose. As a parent, you have to point your child's life toward greater goals than mere happiness and toward someone, God, who can fulfill the inner needs we all have, that material things, in spite of their emotional appeal, cannot fulfill. This is why it is urgent that you give your child a foundation in knowing that God loves them, that God is real, and that a relationship with the living God is the key to a meaningful and happy life.

Why this matters is also that, not only is your child's wellbeing as a human being at stake, but their eternal destiny. If you will pass on to your child a true and deep understanding and experience of the Christian faith, you prepare them for a life of significance, happiness, purpose, and good relationships. That is what every parent wants for their child. You also give them a relationship with

8

the living God that provides them an entrance into eternal life, which is the great promise of the Christian faith. At the foundation of Christian belief, is the promise of eternal life in Jesus Christ. If this is a true promise, and Christianity is confident that it is, you don't want your child to miss out on it. You and they might have a very, very long time to regret not being more conscious of what was at stake. If there is no other reason, this is a very compelling motivation to take the matter of faith in God and the work of Jesus Christ very seriously, both for yourself and your child!

There are many anxieties you may have, as a parent, in relation to religion. Some parents worry about giving their children too much religious training. They have seen people who have "gone off the deep end" about religious things or who have developed some "kooky" ideas about religion. Isn't it better, you might ask, to give my child just a small dose of religious training, so they are not in danger of religious excess? We will talk about this later in this book, but the answer is that it is better to give your child a deep and true experience of and understanding of authentic Christianity, than just a surface exposure. Authentic Christianity is full of balance, depth, wisdom, and grace. In this book, we are going to talk about how to give your child a right and true understanding of the living God. It turns out that you, as their parent, are the best person to teach your child the right things about God, keep them in the center of the spiritual path, and guide them to positive relationships with God and others.

A CRISIS IN THE CHURCH

That Christian parents lose their children from the faith is not only a crisis for parents, but also a crisis for the church. The statistics are not exact in this area, except that they all say that the church is losing its children at a distressing rate. Along with the statistics from the Barna Group, estimates of the number of children who will leave the church, either permanently or for an extended period of time, range from one-third to two-thirds. If any of these numbers are even close to accurate, the magnitude of the problem is alarming in the extreme.

What this means for the church is that, in every generation, the church automatically loses one-third to one-half its membership. Could you imagine investing your money in a company that you knew would lose up to half its value every twenty-five years? You would have to invest huge amounts of money just to stay even.

That is what the church has to do. The church must put tremendous effort into evangelism because of an attrition rate of thirty to fifty percent! This is not to say that evangelism is bad. It is very good. But how much would the church grow if it could keep its children! If the church could keep its children, it would automatically increase its numbers by thirty to fifty percent, instead of struggling just to stay even. There is nothing that would change the church of the future and the world faster than this!

For those who love the church this issue is crucial. There is no more important crisis in the church. The good news however is that the problem is easily fixed. It can be fixed by parents investing time, in the right way, into their child's spiritual life, through a few simple practices. The solution is simple; it only needs to be taught.

Why is the solution simple? Because there is no group more easily influenced than children. It is why Jesus himself said that we must become like little children in order to enter the kingdom of heaven. Children are trusting, naïve, and open. Because they are so open, it is not hard to teach them about God. They respond with belief and trust when taught about the existence and love of God. The good news is that this is not an endeavor that requires church programs, or new curriculum, or rethinking the church's evangelism strategy. It only requires parents to understand and do a few simple things. That is what this book is about.

What is obvious, when we think about it for a moment, is that the church has one first and ready field of evangelism; it is its children. If the church can win over its children, the church of the next generation will change the world in a way it has not done up to this point. This is where Jesus' words find their perfect fulfillment when he said that we should lift up our eyes to see that the field is ripe for the harvest!

We would like the church to reach its potential and move into a new day in which its impact on society will be significant. If you will use the ideas in this book with your children, with your church, and with parents you know, it will change, not only them and the church, but the world, in the next twenty-five years.

A SOLUTION

What we need in order to address this crisis is a plan that is intentional, straightforward, and relatively easy to implement. This is not an area in which parents or the church should be haphazard. In the most important area of a child's spiritual development, there needs to be an intentional method and process, so that faith, penetrates, not just your child's head, but their heart. In this book, I am going to teach you such a method. I believe it possible, as a parent, to pass your faith along to your children, through the simple act of teaching them to pray. By this I do not mean rote prayers or merely teaching them certain rules or methods about prayer. I mean teaching them to develop their own life of prayer. What is so effective about this is that it brings children into their own authentic relationship with the living God. This is the missing piece for most young people, a real and authentic *experience* of the Christian faith. The reality is that, in church they get knowledge about faith, and occasional warm, fuzzy feelings but often not sufficiently impactful experiences of Christianity. That is, in part, because real experiences of faith cannot be manufactured. They are the work of the Holy Spirit, whose workings are full of mystery. He works on his own terms and does not come at our beck and call.

As much as youth programs try to touch the hearts of youth for God, it is surprisingly difficult to do. Faith is not something you can simply pour into a person's heart. You cannot manufacture a real experience of God for someone. An encounter with God is more something that happens to us than something we do. So what can we do, as parents, to help this happen for our children? Is there anything we can do?

The landscape can be very confusing in this regard. Christian parents certainly want to pass their faith along to their children. The question is how? Is the church the answer? Or reading the Bible to them? Or serving others? Or family conversations? What should I do as a parent and where do we start?

All the things I just mentioned are important and have their place. There is a different and better starting point, however. It has to do with prayer. Prayer is the first response of faith to God for every person. When we recognize God in our lives, the first response is to pray, whether a prayer of thanksgiving, a humble confession, or a cry for help.

Because prayer is the basic way we relate to God, this is the place to start with children. If you will teach your child to pray, you enable them to turn their heart toward God and develop their own relationship with the living God. This may sound simple or even simplistic. Surely it cannot be as simple as teaching my child to pray? Yes, it can and it is. I am going to teach you a simple but profound way to connect your child to the living God, naturally and authentically. Prayer has ancient roots, some of which have been mostly lost in today's world. I am going to give you a simple method for helping your child develop their own authentic relationship with God by teaching your child to pray and by your praying with your child. I am going to teach you a natural but profound way to help your child enter into their own experience of

13

the living God through the simple act of praying their own prayers, with you on a regular basis. This practice is so simple that you will be surprised how easy it is for you to do with your child. What I am going to teach you is how to make this the most profound experience of God your child will have and one that will introduce them to the living God.

In saying that the church has not done a good job in passing the faith along to its children, I am not in any way disparaging the work of the church. I am a Christian pastor and love the church. I am only saying that you, as the parent, have the primary role in passing your faith along to your children. Your family's involvement in the church is important and will be a tremendous support to you, but there are things you must do as the parent to ensure that your child "catches" the Christian faith. That is what this book is about.

THE CRITICAL WINDOW OF OPPORTUNITY

There is one little-recognized reality when it comes to passing the Christian faith along to your child. It has to do with a natural window of opportunity that God has given parents. There is a perfect age to pass your Christian faith along to your child. It is between the ages of 3-12. These are the ages in which you have the most influence over your child. If you will use these practices at those ages, you will be amazed at the fruit they will bear.

What we discuss in this book will work with teenagers also, and we have an entire chapter on teenagers, but the perfect window of opportunity is ages 3-12. If your children are already teenagers, there is still hope; you will just have to work a little harder. The perfect age, however, is between 3 and 12. This is when it is relatively easy to build a deep life of faith in your child. If at all possible, you must take advantage of this God-given natural window.

This book is designed to be useful for groups within the church, as well as individual parents. At the end, there are resources for discussion, both between husband and wife, among friends, and in a group setting. There are also links to resources to facilitate group discussions of this material, as this is an ideal topic for church classes and small groups. I would encourage you, not only to use these ideas individually, but share them with others in your neighborhood and church. This book is designed to help you do so in a variety of different settings.

One more comment before we leave this introduction. If you, as a parent, have grown children who have dropped out of the church, all is not lost. If you missed the window of opportunity with your child or children, or for whatever reason, the Christian faith did not stick with your child, there are things you can do. In the Conclusion, I will address this and give you some practical things you can do to nurture your adult child back toward the faith.

With that introduction, let's get started. If you are a Christian parent, this may be the most important book you will ever read. It will make all the difference in your child's life, both now and for eternity. Your child's eternal destiny is at stake so these matters could not be more important. In addition, teaching your child to pray will be one of the most enriching and rewarding experiences of your life. You are going to enjoy this process immensely. So how do we begin? We start with recognizing the importance of your role as a parent and your child's ability to understand spiritual things.

1

RECOGNIZE THE IMPORTANCE OF YOUR ROLE AS A PARENT

LET'S FACE IT, PARENTING IS NOT EASY

PARENTING IS NOT EASY. I once read a plaque that said, "Parenting is like being pecked to death by chickens." This gives a visual image, doesn't it! The difficulty of parenting is the sheer dogged persistence it takes to do it well. A thousand little problems, irritations, and challenges face parents. "Mommy, Amy hit me." "Daddy, can you fix my toy." "Why can't I stay up later?" "I don't want to do my homework." "Can we have some ice cream?" "I don't like Jamie anymore." "I don't want to eat this." And so forth.

In spite of the difficulties, having parents is part of God's grand plan for every child. That a child is born into the arms of two people who think they are the most beautiful thing they have ever seen, is just how God designed it. That children are born into families who absolutely adore them is the way God wants it to be. As parents, we are the people God has ordained to love our children, even in the moments when they are not adorable. We are also the people God has chosen to guide our children into right paths of life and into the way of faith.

The reality is most of us take our job as parents very seriously. We make sure our children get a good night's sleep. Even when they don't want to go to bed, we make them, because we know it's for their good. We feed them a good breakfast, more or less, though, on occasion, there may be a microwave oven or pop tart involved. We try to send them off to school happy, so the morning starts off right. We take them to soccer, baseball, band, piano, art, and other activities. On occasion we take them to the zoo, or the movies, or on vacation, maybe even Disney World! As parents we give our children everything we can think of that will give them good experiences in life and tools with which to succeed, at least as much as our energy level and pocketbook will allow.

But what if? What if we do all these things but neglect the most important job we have as parents? What if we do everything else well but fail to pass along our Christian faith? If that happens, we will have failed at the most important job we have as Christian parents.

WHOSE JOB IS IT?

Whose job is it to teach the faith to our child? Most people think it is the church's. We assume that if we take our children to church, the faith will somehow be assimilated into their mind and heart. This is a natural assumption. The church is supposed to help people understand the faith. Isn't that what will happen with our children; they will become Christians by going to church? Sadly, often no.

The reality is parents *hope* the church will pass the faith along to their child, because they are certain they do not know how. If asked how they should help their child come to know God, most parents have no clue, other than taking their children to church. But this places a great deal of responsibility on the church. Can the church adequately fill this role? More importantly, what if the church fails? Do you want to trust you child's eternal salvation to whether or not your church's youth advisor does a good job? Do you want to give your child's eternal destiny to a youth volunteer or even paid youth pastor who may not really know what they are doing?

This issue is not just theoretical but personal and practical. The issue for every parent of passing the faith along to their child is of utmost importance! Are we going to leave this responsibility to someone else? We should not! God has given *us* the responsibility and we must rise to it. The question is, "How?"

I believe that Christian parents want to pass their faith along to their children; they just don't know how. Should they read them the Bible? Or have religious conversations with them? Or have family devotions? Or tell them Bible stories? Or sit them down and make them memorize Bible verses? What exactly is the process for passing the faith along to your child?

The reason most parents don't know how to pass along their faith is their parents did not do so with them, or did not do so effectively. If your parents were successful in passing the faith along to you, your situation is rare. If your parents did not pass the faith along to you, it is probably because their parents did not pass it along to them. The reason you, as a parent, don't know what to do is because your parents did not do this for you. That they were not good role models in this regard is probably because they did not have a good role model in their parents, who probably did not have good role models in theirs. As we will learn in this book, however, it only takes one generation to break the cycle in a positive direction. If you can effectively pass along your faith, you not only save your child's soul but teach your child how to do the same with their children.

FINDING ROLE MODELS

What instruction does the Bible give us about passing our faith along to our children? While it gives many positive encouragements, it also details many failures. For example, in the Old Testament, when God gave the people the law at Mount Sinai, he specifically instructed parents to teach those laws to their children. Remember God gave the people of Israel the Ten Commandments as they gathered around Mount Sinai. In addition, however, he also gave them many laws, some explaining how to implement the Ten Commandments and others focusing on other aspects of their life as a nation. What were people to do? They were to teach all God's commands and statues to their children.

In *Deuteronomy*, chapter 6, for example, God told people to teach his commands *diligently* to their children. They were to talk about them with their children, when they sat at home, as they walked along, when they rose up, and when they went to sleep. In other words, they were to give great attention to passing God's commands on to their children (*Deuteronomy* 6:7, 11:19). How did the people do in this regard? Rather badly! In fact, they could hardly have failed any worse. The story of the nation of Israel was that succeeding generations regularly forgot to follow God. Even when one generation followed God faithfully, inevitably the next would not. This indicates how poorly parents in the Old Testament passed their faith along to their children.

This is not to say people did not understand the need. The book of *Proverbs* is a wonderful book about the importance of God's wisdom. The first 9 chapters, before the proverbs actually begin, are a father's instructions to his son about the importance of God's ways. These chapters come from Solomon himself and are his encouragement to his own son. What does he say? He encourages his son to listen to his father's advice, so he will learn wisdom. In addition, the son is not to forsake his mother's teaching either. The instruction of your parents will be a graceful garland around your neck, says Solomon, if you will only give heed. This section is summarized in the verse that encourages the son, "Be not wise in your own eyes; fear the Lord and turn away from evil." (*Proverbs* 3:7) For parents, these chapters extol the importance of passing wisdom and instruction along to your children.

How well did Solomon teach his children? Not well, as it turned out. The words of Solomon are good ones, but his own example would be one of failure. The son who would follow after him as king, Rehoboam, would act foolishly and immediately lose more than half the kingdom. We might wonder how it is Solomon did not train his children better, especially the one to whom he would entrust the throne? The answer is probably complex, but some things are clear. One is Solomon had too many children to manage. With 700 wives, Solomon had more children than he could count. With that many children, he could not have remembered all their names, much less spent time nurturing them. It was one of the reasons God told kings not to multiply wives to themselves. With too many children, you simply cannot train them in righteous living. At some point the inmates begin running the asylum. For all Solomon's good advice about training children, he failed to take it himself, to the detriment of his family and the nation.

A POSITIVE ROLE MODEL

Where do we find a positive role model in the Bible? One place to look is the example of Paul's young ministry companion, Timothy. Timothy was a young man whom the apostle Paul met on his second missionary journey when he came to the town of Lystra (*Acts* 16:1-3). Timothy had a sincere faith and many gifts for ministry, so Paul took Timothy along with him as a ministry companion. He would become part of the team that ministered with Paul and someone Paul trusted to faithfully teach and preach. On a number of occasions, Paul would send Timothy to various churches to check on their needs. Timothy's name is also listed as a "co-author" for the letters of *II Corinthians, Philippians, Colossians, Philemon,* and *I* and *II Thessalonians*. Two letters in the New Testament, *I* and *II Timothy*, are written specifically to Timothy to give him instruction and encouragement.

How then did Timothy come to an authentic faith? We get some indication in the first chapter of Paul's second letter to Timothy. We see Paul's affection for Timothy in this chapter, for he calls him his "beloved child," meaning his spiritual child in the faith. Paul then comments on Timothy's sincere faith, which he says was first found in his grandmother Lois and also in his mother Eunice. What was the importance of Timothy's mother and grandmother in his spiritual development? Apparently, they were very important because later in *II Timothy* (3:15), Paul will remind Timothy how he had known the sacred scriptures, which are able to make him wise for salvation, from his youth. Since Timothy's father was Greek and apparently a pagan, Timothy's faith came through his mother, who was Jewish, and her mother as well.

What does this mean? It is an example of a family in which faith was effectively passed along from one generation to the next. It is also important to note that is was done in a situation in which only one parent believed. This ought to be encouragement to those whose spouse is either not present or less interested in matters of faith than you are. We will say more about this later, but at this point we should note that one parent is able to pass the faith along to their children, if they are intentional about doing so. If you are a single parent, be encouraged. There is a great deal that you can do.

What did Timothy's mother and grandmother do to pass their faith along to Timothy? The information we have does not tell us exactly. We do learn that they taught Timothy the scriptures. Paul sees this as very important because, in his words, the scriptures are able to make people "wise for salvation." What seems clear is that Timothy's mother and grandmother gave attention to his spiritual life from an early age.

THE POWER OF YOUR INFLUENCE

One more story before we leave this chapter. The book of *Acts*, chapter 16, recounts Paul's experience in the city of Philippi. Because Paul had cast a demon out of a girl who used her abilities to tell fortunes, her owners had Paul and Silas beaten and thrown into prison. *Acts* tells how Paul and Silas began to sing and pray at midnight. This must have seemed odd to the other prisoners and especially the jailer who knew how badly they had been beaten. How could they find joy in their condition when they were not only hurting badly but in the deepest part of the prison? God obviously heard their prayers however, because, as they prayed and sang, an earthquake came, shaking the entire prison. So powerful was it that the prison doors came open and, miraculously, the chains of all the prisoners came loose.

Paul might have seen this as an opportunity from God to escape, but he did not. In fact, the jailer had awoken with the earthquake and assumed that everyone had escaped. As his life depended on guarding the prisoners, he had drawn his sword and was preparing to kill himself, rather than be tortured for losing those in his care. Paul however realized what was happening and called out. "Do not harm yourself, for we are all here." The jailer rushed in to find that it was true. His prisoners were all still there. *Acts* says that in great anxiety, he said to Paul and Silas, "What must I do to be saved?" They took his words to mean more than just keeping his prisoners from escaping. They replied, "Believe in the Lord Jesus, and you will be saved, you and your household."

Acts then says that the jailer, after securing the prison again, no doubt, took Paul and Silas to his home. He washed their wounds and gave them something to eat. We do not have all the details of what happened, but Paul and Silas apparently explained to them the good news of Jesus because it says that the jailer and his entire household rejoiced that they had come to believe in God.

25

There are a couple of important things to notice about this story. One is the influence of the jailer on his entire household. His faith would impact, not just himself but his entire family. This is also true for us as. As a parent, we are in a role in which we can make a tremendous impact on our entire family, particularly in the matter of faith. If we will believe and live out that faith, it will change the entire dynamic of our family life. We are going to talk about exactly how to do this as we go along.

Also notice Paul's words to the jailer. He told him that if he would believe in Jesus Christ, not only would he be saved but his entire household. This is a tremendous promise! God's grace is not just for us but also for our family. God's promises extend beyond ourselves to our children. God wants our entire household to be saved. Against the current statistics, God's intention is for you not to lose any of your children but for them all to grow up into mature, healthy, authentic Christian disciples. This is a promise from God and one we want to appropriate for ourselves and our family.

A Tremendous Opportunity

Christian parents certainly want to pass their faith along to their children; in most instances, they are simply not sure how. For example, they do not know how to enter into natural conversations about spiritual things in a way that is not forced or awkward. If they could find a way, however, more parents would do so. But what is that way? How can you have natural conversations with your child about God? This is what we are going to answer in this book.

There is a reason many parents do not engage their children in spiritual conversations. It is an embarrassing reason. Many parents, quite frankly, are afraid of the questions they will get asked. What if my child asks a religious question I don't know how to answer? I don't want to be embarrassed and let them know how little I know about the faith. I also don't want to give them a wrong answer to something. For this reason, many parents avoid conversations about religious things with their children. This is too bad because children have many questions and need answers. As it turns out, you, as their parent, are the perfect person to answer their questions, even if the idea makes you nervous.

If this is one of your anxieties, there is good news. There are good ways to answer your child's religious questions and we will talk about this in detail in later chapters. You will be surprised at how easy it turns out to be to answer most of your child's questions, even the seemingly difficult ones.

I hope you are seeing a picture here. You as the parent have a tremendous opportunity to impact your child's life for God and for good. Just because others may not have done this well in the past, does not mean you cannot. Just because your parents did not effectively pass the faith along to you does not mean that you cannot to your children. In fact, we are going to help you become an effective spiritual leader in your home, even if you don't feel like you are one now. You will be surprised how easy this is.

There is one more topic we need to examine in the beginning. It is the question of what kind of spiritual aptitude children have. How much religious instruction are children able to absorb? This becomes an important question when we begin to consider when to start the spiritual training of our children. This is what we will examine in the next chapter. Can children develop real spiritual understanding?

2

CAN CHILDREN LEARN SPIRITUAL THINGS?

THE ABILITY OF CHILDREN TO LEARN

IN THE LAST CHAPTER, we talked about your role, as a parent, in passing your faith along to your children. We made a surprising and perhaps disconcerting assertion. It was that it is not the church's job to pass the Christian faith along to your child. Or your child's Sunday School teacher. Or small group leader. Or youth pastor. The job of passing the Christian faith along to your child is *yours* as your child's parent. *Deuteronomy* 6 is very clear about this. Parents are to teach their children about God, when they rise in the morning, when they sit at meals, when they walk along, and when they lie down in the evening. Paul, in *Ephesians*, instructs fathers to raise their children in the discipline and instruction of the Lord. If we read the Bible closely, this responsibility is clear. If you are a parent, the job of passing the faith along to your child belongs, first and foremost, to you.

The question, of course, is how to do it. One common misconception is that we ought to wait until our children become teenagers to really engage them with spiritual matters. After all, isn't this when young people begin to be able to make meaningful life decisions? Don't many people make faith commitments during the teenage years? While these things may be true, this approach misses a unique opportunity God has given parents to impact their child's spiritual development. God does not want your child to have to wait until they are a teenager to begin thinking about God. No, the first and great window of opportunity that God has given you, as a parent, is when your child is young. This is the time when you can impact their lives in a way that will change them forever. But that begs a question. Can children really learn about spiritual things? Do they have the capacity? Is it realistic to start our children young on their journey of faith?

There is an old video that you can find on the internet that demonstrates children's abilities to learn. It is a famous episode of the Mike Douglas show. Mike Douglas was a popular daytime talk show host many years ago. One day a father and son were on the show. The son had a gift for hitting a golf ball. What was remarkable about this episode was that the young boy was only two years old. There was a screen set up into which the young boy could hit a golf ball. Bob Hope, who was an avid golfer was also there. What became quickly evident is that this two-year old boy had a great golf swing. It made for a cute segment and everyone got a kick out of it. Little did anyone know how prophetic that moment would be? The little boy's name was Tiger Woods.

In this chapter, I want to drive home the point, no pun intended, that children have great abilities to learn. We ought to take advantage of that window of opportunity. Why did many successful sports stars begin learning their sport at an early age? The answer is, to develop good muscle memory! They started developing good muscle memory at ages 5 and 6, and sometimes even younger. Hitting a golf ball, or baseball, or tennis ball became second nature. No wonder as adults they can do it better than 99.9% of the rest of the world.

Most of us, even if we start young are not going to develop the muscle memory that Tiger Woods has. He shot a 48 at age 2 on a 9-hole course. He won a 10 and under tournament at age, 3. Very impressive! But here is the question: If we start children young, can they develop "spiritual muscle memory?" What if we could help our children develop "spiritual muscle memory?" I believe we can. I believe that by starting them early in the practice of prayer, we can help prayer become a natural part of the way they see themselves, understand God, and experience the world. I believe we can make it such a part of their lives that when they grow up, their lives will feel incomplete without it.

This is not psychological manipulation, nor is it simply teaching them a set of skills. Prayer teaches us to align our lives with the living God. If life is meant to be lived in relationship with God, and Christianity believes that it is, then our life only functions well when we keep it connected with God. The way we do this is to

31

pray and wouldn't it be something if we could make prayer for our children as natural as breathing, or as natural as swinging a golf club to Tiger Woods, by starting them early in the practice? That is what I am going to help you do in this series. There is no better thing you can do for your child because by doing this, you help them make a relationship with God a natural part of how they view themselves, how they feel about the world, and what they believe to be true. The value of this cannot be overstated!

CAN CHILDREN PRAY IN A MEANINGFUL WAY?

If it is true that children can learn spiritual things even when they are young, there ought to be stories about this in the Bible. As it turns out, there are a couple of very important stories about children, prayer, and faith. One of these is the account of Palm Sunday. Palm Sunday begins the final week of Jesus' life and ministry. He had been traveling slowly toward Jerusalem from Galilee, along with many pilgrims, as they journeyed to the capital city for the greatest religious festival of the year, the Passover. What only Jesus knew was that this would be the final week of his life. So important is this event in the life of Jesus that it is recorded in all four gospels.

Jesus came into the city on that first Palm Sunday from the eastern side of the city. There was a small mountain, the Mount of Olives, that you had to cross to enter the city from that direction. Early that morning, Jesus and his disciples came over the mountain with Jesus riding on a donkey. There was a lot of irony in Jesus' manner of entrance. Jesus came into the city as its long awaited Messiah and King. Yet he did not enter as Caesar would have, with soldiers and swords, riding on a great stallion. Jesus entered humbly, riding on a donkey, as the Old Testament prophets said the Messiah would.

When a person stood on the peak of the Mount of Olives, they were presented with a magnificent view of the city of Jerusalem. Jesus and his disciples would have looked down into the city and directly onto the magnificent temple of Herod, its gold and white marble gleaming in the morning sun. What happened next was unexpected and spontaneous. The followers of Jesus in the city heard that Jesus was approaching. They streamed out of the city in great numbers to greet his arrival. As he came down the side of the Mount of Olives, they began to acclaim Jesus King and Messiah. "Hosanna in the highest," they shouted, waving palm branches and throwing their cloaks on the ground in front of Jesus. "Blessed is the one who comes in the name of the Lord. Hosanna!" The celebration was boisterous and enthusiastic, with both children and adults shouting. When the religious leaders demanded that Jesus stop the people's acclamations, Jesus replied that if they were to be silent, the stones themselves would cry out.

What does this have to do with children? As it turns out, there were children present on that first Palm Sunday. This is not surprising because people came to the festivals in family groups. From the accounts in the gospels, we discover that, on that day, along with the adults, the children waved palm branches too. Like

33

the adults, they were part of the procession. They also did one other important thing. Like their parents, they shouted the praises of Jesus. The Gospel of *Luke* reports that they shouted, "Hosanna to the Son of David!" We know this because the religious leaders took note of it and protested. They objected that the children were shouting Jesus' praises and proclaiming him the Messiah.

The religious leaders, of course, did not believe in Jesus. They were sure that the Messiah, when he came, would be very different than Jesus. That even the children were shouting Jesus' praises and proclaiming him king of the nation was too much for them. They utterly despised Jesus by this point in his ministry. So, when Jesus arrived at the temple, the religious leaders came to him with an angry complaint. "How dare you allow these *children* to sing your praises? Don't you hear what they are saying? Stop them immediately."

What did Jesus do? Nothing. He would not stop the children from praising him. In fact, the children's words were completely appropriate. Jesus responded and said to the religious leaders, "Have you never read how the prophet said, 'Out of the mouth of infants and nursing babies, you have prepared praise?'" In other words, the children's praises were completely appropriate and acceptable to Jesus. They were right on the mark and Jesus would not stop them. Jesus accepted their praises just as he did the praises of their parents. Like their parents, the children praised Jesus well.

This is an instance of children in the Bible praying in a way that was acceptable to Jesus. Praise is a form of prayer and that is exactly what the children were doing, they were praising God and

34

apparently quite well, for Jesus commended them. Their words may simply have been an imitation of what their parents modeled for them, but they were appropriate and acceptable to Jesus.

This gives us an example from which we can learn. Our children's prayers do not have to be sophisticated to be acceptable to God. Our children do not need to pray with the understanding that we have. They do not need to have a degree in theology to pray acceptably. Children pray like children. That is the beauty of their prayers. Their prayers are full of belief and trust. They do not worry about the same things adults do. They pray with honest hearts and willing spirits. In some instances our children will probably pray better than we do.

Palm Sunday is an instance of children praying acceptably in the sight of Jesus. If the praises of the children on Palm Sunday were acceptable to Jesus, we should not doubt that *our* children can pray acceptable prayers also. If we will teach our children to pray, even though their prayers may not always be sophisticated, those prayers will be acceptable to God.

CAN CHILDREN LEARN SPIRITUAL THINGS?

There is another story in the Bible that helps us understand how children can develop spiritual understanding. It is the story of Jesus in the temple as a boy. *The Gospel of Luke* gives us the only account of the life of Jesus as a child. The story is found in *Luke* 2:41-52 and happened when Jesus was twelve years old. The family, including the relatives, had been to one of the great festivals in the city of Jerusalem. There were festivals each year to which families traveled together. These were times of worship, relaxation, and fellowship. For a week the family worshipped together, enjoyed each other's company, and got needed rest from their regular labors.

When the festival was over, Mary and Joseph left Jerusalem to return home with their relatives and extended family. The entire group left to make the journey north to Nazareth and Jesus's parents assumed Jesus was with his cousins. But Jesus was not; he had stayed behind in the city. We might find it strange that Mary and Joseph did not know where he was, but people traveled in large extended families to these festivals, so they must have assumed that Jesus was with his friends and the relatives. At that point, Mary and Joseph had a bundle of other children to watch after and Jesus was not the one most likely to be caught trying to take one of the camels for a spin on his own, when no one was looking.

But when Jesus didn't show up for dinner, Mary and Joseph's pulses began to race. Not only did they obviously care about their son, but you would hate to be the parents who "lost" the Messiah! Back to Jerusalem they raced. Three days they searched frantically around the city calling his name. "Jesus, where are you," and saying to people, 'Have you seen a young boy named Jesus around here?" Finally someone suggested they look in the temple and there he was, sitting calmly in the middle of a crowd of the teachers of the law. He was sitting with them, looking right at home, listening to them, and asking questions. *Luke* reports that all who heard him were amazed at his understanding and his answers. "Where did this lad get this

36

depth of understanding," they wondered, which was not exactly Mary and Joseph's primary reaction to Jesus' disappearance!

This is a revealing story from the life of Jesus and it tells us what a good job Mary and Joseph were doing with Jesus. They had given him religious training that was serving him well. But there is something more to be noticed here. Part of what we learn from this story is that children, for Jesus certainly was one at the time, are able to understand spiritual things. Jesus did not suddenly and instantly gain all this understanding at age twelve. His understanding at age twelve was evidence that he had been learning scripture, reflecting on it, and thinking about God for some time, probably since an early age.

Admittedly Jesus was unusual, to say the least, so his example sets the bar higher than any of us can reach. But this story is revealing about both children and a parent's role. The fact that, by age twelve, Jesus had a significant grasp of spiritual matters ought to serve as encouragement to us as parents. Our children can grasp more than we think they can. If we will teach them about God, they can develop real, true, and meaningful understandings about God. For that reason, we should not "lose" the years of their childhood and wait until they are teenagers to begin to teach them about God. Mary and Joseph certainly did not. That Jesus was able to sit with the religious leaders in the temple was evidence, not only of his divine wisdom, but also of a childhood full of scripture, instruction, and prayer. Since children absorb things so readily during their childhood years, it is the perfect time to teach them about God.

Here then is a practical principle of parenting; children can learn about spiritual things and even learn to pray. We ought to do everything in our power to make it easy for them to do so. The added bonus that occurs when we teach our children to pray is that we not only instruct them in the things of God but also help them come to *know* God. Prayer is the perfect vehicle to help our children come to *know* God.

PARENTAL ANXIETIES

As we said in the introduction, the idea of teaching your child about God may raise your parental anxieties. You may worry if this is something you can really do? "Can I teach my child about God? I don't know that much about God or the Christian faith myself? How can I teach someone else?" It certainly might be the case that you do not have a sophisticated understanding of the Christian faith. Your anxiety, therefore, might not be completely unfounded. For that reason, you may need to do some things to get up to speed in your own understanding of the faith.

The reality is that it is easy to stay at a kindergarten level in our understanding of the faith. If we went to church when we were young, we learned the stories about Noah and the Ark, David and Goliath, and Jesus in the boat with the disciples. But many times, people get disconnected from the church for a period of time. During this time their spiritual learning goes on hiatus or even into hibernation. When they start having children, however, they realize they need to get back to church. They want their kids to grow up in church. It was a good experience for them. It is part of what they think will make for a healthy family life. Of course, they are right about all this.

At this point, when people come back to church, they often have their Vacation Bible School lessons and not much more. They have pieces of things, bits of information, and various stories from the Bible, but it's all jumbled up. If that is your situation, there is good news. Being part of this study is a great first step to getting up to speed in your Christian education. You are going to learn a lot about what Christians believe in this book. We are going to help you know how to answer your children's religious questions. We will also point you to other resources at the end to help jumpstart your faith and understanding.

To go back to one of our original questions, is it really important for you, as a parent, to teach your children about God? Is it really important to put effort into their religious training? The answer is a resounding, "Yes!" Your child's religious development is too important to leave to someone else. It is your job as their parent to take responsibility in this area.

This makes perfect sense, if we think about it. We understand that our children need to be taught when it comes to such things as science, reading, and math. We know that a good teacher is a great help in learning. With a good teacher, one can learn the accumulated knowledge of previous generations much faster than if one is left to figure it out by oneself. Imagine thinking that our child ought to be left to figure out algebra or grammar or geography by themselves.

We teach these disciplines so we do not have to recreate the things others have learned over the centuries. We don't expect our children to develop the Pythagorean theorem all by themselves. We teach it to them so they can go even further along in their understanding of math.

If this is true in ordinary educational subjects, shouldn't it be true in spiritual things? Should we leave our child to figure out basic Christian disciplines and practices on their own? Of course not, especially when we can teach them things that will move them forward in their life of faith.

Many parents leave their children to their own devices when it comes to figuring out spiritual things and some children are able to do so, but many will not. You can help your child in a significant way by teaching them, so they move steadily along the path of faith, prayer, and life with God. Just as we don't start our children in school at age thirteen, we don't want to start our child's religious training then either. We want to help them early on by imparting the accumulated knowledge of the Christian faith as soon as possible. This is what we are going to help you be able to do, naturally and successfully.

WHAT HAPPENS WHEN PEOPLE PRAY?

What you do with your child, in teaching them to pray, is crucially important because something happens when people pray. This is what Christians believe. Prayer gets us in touch with the

40

living God, who is real, and who really acts in people's lives. God answers our prayers, many times in ways we can recognize if we are paying attention. It is great to ask God for what we need and have God answer.

But there is something more. In addition to answers of various types, something else happens. When people pray with an honest and open heart, and children certainly do that, they *experience God*. It is as simple as that. They experience the presence of God warming their hearts. Over time, they begin to know what being close to God feels like. They sense in their spirits that God is near and that their life has a foundation that is much deeper than themselves. This is key for you to understand and I cannot overstate the importance of this. If you will teach your child to pray, you will usher him or her into the real presence of God.

Let me share a story about one of the many ways I observed this as we taught our children to pray. One of the things people often have a hard time saying is, "I love you." This is especially true for men. I try to tell my wife and boys that I love them on a regular basis, but it has been a learned skill. This was certainly true when it came to God. I respected God and wanted to serve God. After all, I was a pastor. But I generally did not tell God I loved him. Was this the kind of thing you said to God? Of course, I felt a true devotion to God and did love God, but should you tell God you loved him? That sort of thing seemed awfully "mushy." Besides, if you were going to tell God you loved him, actually say it, you had better mean it! It was not something one ought to say to God lightly.

I noticed at one point, however, that several people whose faith I respected used the phrase often. When they told God they loved him, it seemed natural. I knew they meant it; it was not trite or superficial. It came from the heart and seemed to express a deep emotional affection for God. Of course, the first great commandment is to *love God* with your heart and mind and soul and strength. So I decided to try to use the phrase more often and see if I could gain a comfort level with telling God I loved him. If I meant it, then why not say it!

About this time I was beginning to say nighttime prayers with each of our boys. A brainstorm came to me one night. We would all begin to close our prayers with the simple phrase, "Dear God, I love you very much." I instructed each of the boys that we would end our prayers every night with that phrase. I did not make a big deal about it. I just said that this was what we were going to start doing. They were young enough to simply accept this idea and we all began doing so.

I do not remember this being particularly uncomfortable for them, only for myself. But as the weeks went by, I found myself much more at ease with this closing to our nighttime prayers. "Dear God, I love you very much." The boys were apparently very comfortable with the phrase. They said it as if it were just how everyone closed their prayers. I suppose they assumed that everyone told God they loved him; it was just what people did when they prayed. And it became just what *we* did when *we* prayed. It dawned on me however, that something very important was happening. The idea that they loved God was becoming a natural part both of their

42

prayers, and here is the key, of their very persons. That is, it was becoming a natural part of their belief about themselves. They were people who loved God.

I have since developed a philosophy about this. It is this. If a person says that they love God long enough, they will begin to believe it and if they believe it, they will feel it. *Say it in order to believe it; believe it in order to feel it.* This may sound a bit like weak pop psychology, but it is not. It is an ancient principle of the spiritual life. The ancient Christian mystics said, "It begins on the lips, then enters the mind, then finally is embraced by the heart."

I began to realize that I had stumbled on an ancient principle of the spiritual life, which is that it takes time for certain beliefs to move from our minds into our hearts. If you want something you believe, or want to believe, to enter your heart, start it on the lips. Say it in words. From your words, it will enter more firmly into your mind. As it repeatedly comes from your lips and takes hold in your mind, it will be embraced by your heart. This is a way of moving intellectual beliefs from simply dry propositions to the place where we embrace them with passion. One night one of our children added his own words to our closing phrase. He said, with feeling, "Dear God, I love you *very, very, very, very much.*" He meant it and felt it and I knew that something very special was happening.

In teaching your child to pray, they are not entering into an indifferent relationship with God. They are not simply learning a skill. They are not going through the motions. You are going to teach them to love God, not just with their head but their heart. I am going to help you teach your child to love God *very, very, very, very much.*

3

UNDERSTAND THE NATURE AND PRACTICE OF PRAYER PART ONE

WHAT IS PRAYER?

IN THE FIRST TWO CHAPTERS, we have begun to lay the groundwork to help you pass the Christian faith along to your child through the simple practice of teaching them to pray. But can you really teach your child how to pray? Can the average person understand prayer well enough to teach it?

Somewhere in your studies, you may have heard the name of the ancient Greek philosopher, Plato. He was the second of the three great Greek philosophers of the 4th and 5th centuries B.C., along with Socrates and Aristotle. Plato taught on a wide variety of subjects

45

and had a clear sense of what it took to be a good teacher. Interestingly, it wasn't having a gift for teaching nor was it being a good talker. Being a good teacher had nothing to do with eloquence or charisma. Plato understood that the most important thing a person needed in order to teach a subject, was to understand the subject. The first order of business is to understand what we want to teach.

This applies to us as parents as we consider the prospect of teaching our children to pray. If we are going to teach our child to pray, we first need to have a solid understanding of the practice of prayer. In addition to being a person who prays, it will be helpful if we have some language to talk about prayer, understand some principles of prayer, and are able to think rationally about why we do certain things when we pray. You don't necessarily need to be an expert on every aspect of prayer. You don't have to be able to teach about prayer on a college level, just be a little bit ahead of your child. With what you learn in this chapter and the next, you will have everything you need to be comfortable in talking to your child about prayer and teaching them what they need to know to get started.

Let's start with a definition. A simple definition of prayer is that it is conversation with God. This is a way you can explain it to your child. Prayer is simply conversation with God. When we pray, we talk to God. If you think about it, this definition has a profound assumption behind it. It assumes that God *wants* to be in conversation with us. Think about that! Does God really want to talk to us? Some people believe God may be out there, but he is silent.

They believe he doesn't talk to us and doesn't listen when we talk to him. Is that the case?

Imagine God as a parent, however. God certainly is a parent, since he created us. Do you think God, as a parent, would create the universe, make a world such as ours, create us in his image and likeness, then refuse to talk to us? Do you refuse to talk to your child? Of course, not. We *talk* to our children. And we want them to talk to us! Occasionally we may want them to talk less, but that is another matter. Does it make sense that God would create humans then refuse to speak to them? The answer of Christianity is, "No!" The witness of the Bible throughout is that God is not silent. He makes himself known to his creation. He speaks and invites us to listen. Jesus himself said, "Let anyone who has ears listen." God also invites us to speak to him and promises that he will listen when we do. How about that!

What then is prayer? It is talking with a God who wants to interact with us and listen to us. Notice that this definition of prayer affirms that God has personhood. That is a basic but important concept. By this I mean that God is not an impersonal force, like "May the Force be with you." You can't have a conversation with a force, or something without personhood. Think about the fact that the Star Wars Jedi's don't ever actually talk to The Force. That is because, in the Star Wars "universe," the Force is an "energy field" but not something with personhood. You cannot have conversation with a rock, or tree, or a force, such as electricity or magnetism. If you do, they generally don't make much of a response! Conversation happens between persons.

Prayer assumes the personhood of God. This doesn't mean that God is exactly like we are. It simply means that God thinks, feels, loves, values, and communicates. These are things persons do and we do these things because we are made in God's likeness. *We* get these attributes from God. God is both the Creator of all things and someone with whom we can have a *personal* relationship. How do we have a personal relationship with God? The answer is, through prayer.

Christianity affirms that humans have a real relationship with God because God has created us to be able to do so. When we pray, it is not just something that happens in our minds or imaginations; when we pray, we really commune with the living God.

The indication of God's desire for relationship with us is that he created us in his image and likeness. It is this characteristic that makes it possible for us to commune with him. As electrical wires are made for the purpose of carrying current, we are made to be in a relationship with God. According to the Bible, only humans are made with this capacity.

How then is God truly real to us? The answer is, "through the Holy Spirit." Christianity affirms that God gives his Holy Spirit to those who believe in Jesus Christ. On the Day of Pentecost, God's Spirit came to be present with his people, by being among them and within them. The belief that God lives within us through his Spirit is called the "indwelling" of the Holy Spirit. God's Spirit comes to indwell us, unite with our spirits, make us children of God, give us a new heart full of love for God, and help us sense and know God's presence in our lives. Through the Holy Spirit, we *experience* the

48

presence of God as a reality in our lives. For that reason, we do not have to go anywhere to pray to God, only open our hearts to him.

THANKSGIVING AND PRAISE

Where should we start when we pray? One classic way to begin is by saying, "Thank you" to God for his blessings. This is a first important element of prayer; part of good prayer takes time to say thank you to God for his gifts. If we think about it, this is good manners, if nothing else. We teach our children to say thank you when someone has done something for them. We make them write a note or send a text or say, "Thank you," in person. It is good to *be* thankful, but we generally think we ought to *say*, "Thank you," as well. We ought to do so with God also.

A famous preacher of the 19th century, Charles Spurgeon, noted that we cannot remember to thank God for everything, but we can remember to thank him for some things. He was making reference to *Psalm* 103:2, which says, "Bless the Lord, O my soul, and forget not all his benefits." He noted that we cannot remember all God's benefits, but we should not *forget* them all either. We can remember *some* of our blessings and prayers of thanksgiving are a way to do this. When we pray, part of what we ought to do is spend time thanking God. If we spent more time thanking God for his blessings, and less time worrying about our troubles, we would be a lot happier and less grumpy.

A first basic kind of prayer then is thanksgiving. There is a second and related type of prayer; it is called "praise," or "adoration." The Bible often says things like, "Praise the Lord, O my soul." "Let all God's people praise him." But what exactly is praise? The answer is that praise focuses more on who God is, rather than what God has done for us. On the first Palm Sunday, the people praised God. They said, "Hosanna. Blessed is the One who comes in the name of the Lord. Blessed is the Son of David." They were praising God for his mercy and goodness in sending the Messiah to them.

Saying that praise focuses more on who God is than what God has done may seem to be a small distinction, but it is important. When we praise God, we are adoring God's majesty, grace, patience, power, mercy, and goodness, more than specific things God has done for us. These are not so much, "Lord, thank you that I avoided that accident yesterday," or "Thank you that some extra money came in so we can pay the bills," but "Thank you Lord, that you love us with an everlasting love and that you never forsake us. We love you and thank you and praise you." The word we often use for these kinds of expressions of gratitude toward God is "worship."

As it turns out, there is no absolute distinction between praise and thanksgiving. They often run together and while we can distinguish between the two, it isn't that important to try to separate them, when we pray. In fact we would hope that our prayers of thanksgiving would often become prayers of praise. In the Bible when people found themselves in the presence of God, their immediate reaction was to be overcome with a sense of awe and

50

unworthiness. They felt the need to confess their sins and fall on their faces in worship. Sometimes when we pray, we become especially aware of God's presence. We feel God's Spirit. These moments especially invite us into praise and worship.

Do we only praise God when we have a certain feeling of awe or when we sense the majesty of God? No. Praise does not have to be a response to a certain feeling when we pray. We need to intentionally lift our hearts to God in adoration in a regular way. In worship, we lift our inner person to God. We let go just a bit of our rational selves and give as much as we know of ourselves back to God. Sometimes we may even seem to lose ourselves in God, just a bit. I hope you will try to make this a part of your life of prayer. Sometimes when you pray, let yourself go. Allow yourself to be caught up in the wonder of who God is. Praise God, thank him, and adore him. The reality is that praise is as close to pure worship as we probably ever get. Whether you begin with praise and thanksgiving, or end with them, they are important parts of a healthy life of prayer.

PRAYERS OF CONFESSION

We have talked so far about two basic types of prayer, thanksgiving and praise. A next aspect of prayer to consider is prayers of confession. What place does confession have in our prayers? The answer is that it has an important place because one of the universal aspects of human behavior is that we are sinful. No one lives up, even to their own aspirations and the Bible says that we all fall short of God's standards. No one keeps God's commandments perfectly; in fact, we fall exceedingly short of them. Our failures may be big or little compared to others, but others are not the standard by which we are measured. The standard is God's laws. The book of *Romans* says simply, "All have sinned and fall short of the glory of God." This is a recognition of our basic sinful human condition before God.

This might sound a bit depressing, but it is crucially important for us to understand, especially as it pertains to prayer, because prayer is one of the places we *confess* our sins and receive *forgiveness*. As Christians, we have someone to forgive us, and this is crucial for us to understand. It is one of the healing and life-changing things that Christianity brings to the human soul. We have someone to forgive us! From a Christian point of view, the way we know that we are sinful is to compare our selves to God's laws in the Bible. Society does not determine what is right and wrong because even human laws can be misguided. There is a heavenly Lawgiver, who is the source of right and wrong. God's laws in the Bible have been given us to help us know what is morally right and good in his sight.

God has also given us an inner compass, that is, a conscience. If we do wrong, we feel bad. There is no way to do wrong and feel good. Our consciences will not allow it, though we can desensitize our consciences through misuse over time. The only way to feel good is to do good. But God is slow to anger. When we sin, God waits for us, and our conscience bothers us. When we turn back to

God and ask forgiveness, God washes us clean by his grace. These prayers that ask forgiveness are called prayers of confession.

These kinds of prayers are important both for us and our children. We want our child to develop a sensitive conscience. We want them to be bothered when they do something wrong, and we want them to develop a humble attitude toward God. This is one reason this kind of prayer is important. We need to teach our children to ask God's forgiveness, because we want them to develop a sensitive conscience before God. We want them to know, inside, when they have done something wrong. We want them to be aware of their inner compass and one of the ways we help them cultivate this is to teach them that we all need to ask God to forgive us for our sins. Over the course of this series we will talk about how help your child acquire a soft heart before God.

What then does it take to be forgiven? Do we need to confess every sin in order to be forgiven? The answer of Christianity is, "No." Through Jesus Christ, we have forgiveness for *all* our sins, even those we do not realize we have committed. The truth is, we cannot remember all our sins, nor do we realize all the ways we fall short of God's commandments. For that reason, our forgiveness does not depend on our prayers of confession. The grace of God is such that he invites us to place our faith in Jesus Christ and his sacrifice for us on the cross. God promises complete forgiveness to all who will do so. This is a great gift, the importance of which cannot be overstated. In Jesus Christ, we are forgiven all our sins, past, present, and future.

What then is the purpose of prayers of confession? They help us conform our lives, in increasing ways, to the will of God. They help us recognize our failures in order to correct them. They are also ways in which God cleanses our hearts and spirits. Think of what Christ does for us as being like a medicine that cures a great disease. Through Christ, we are saved from death and given God's healing balm that reunites us with God and gives us eternal life. What then are prayers of confession? Think of them like taking a bath. Though we have been healed of a great disease, we still need to take a bath regularly. Prayers of confession provide cleansing for our spirits so that moral dirt does not accumulate in our lives.

THE PRAYER OF FAITH

One more thing about this before we move on. It may be that you have never personally asked God to forgive you for your sins. You may have heard about the idea or thought about it but not actually done so. If that is the case, this is a good opportunity to stop for a moment to ask God to forgive you your sins. Forgiveness for our sins is the great promise of the Christian faith. Is this important? It is. The Bible teaches that sin is the great barrier between us and God. When Adam and Eve fell from grace, it broke humanity's perfect communion with God. Because of that, every person is in a broken relationship with God, their sins standing between them and God. Because of this broken relationship, we are now at odds with

God. The Bible says that we are, in fact, enemies of God and his anger is directed toward us because of those sins.

Our natural inclination is to think that we just need to try harder to be good and please God. If we can be a good person, we can overcome this problem. But this turns out to be impossible. Once we sin, like Adam and Eve, we break our communion with God. Sin creates such a gap between us and God that it can never be bridged by our efforts, no matter how sincere. The Bible says that a solution was needed that goes beyond our abilities.

What would that solution be? Christianity says that God chose to bring a solution to us by extending us his mercy and grace. God did for us what we could not do for ourselves, provide a way to be reconciled with him. God did this through sending his Son into the world to become a way for our relationship with God to be healed. What we could not do, be perfect, Jesus did. He came and lived a perfect life, then gave his sinless life on the cross for our sakes. Since he was perfect, he could die, not for his own sins, but for the sins of others. Jesus gave his life on the cross as a sacrifice in our place, to pay the penalty for our sins. Jesus experienced physical death so we would not have to experience an eternal death apart from God. Because he was the eternal Son of God, his sacrifice on the cross was of such value that it could pay for the sins of all humankind, past, present, and future.

This is the great message of Christianity. God has come to us to reconcile us to himself. This reconciliation is not something we can do through our own effort. It does not come through our being good or performing certain religious acts. It comes through God's gift of

55

his Son who has made a way for us to be forgiven, redeemed, and made children of God.

How then do we receive this salvation? What God requires of us is both simple and hard. It is simple in that all that is required is that we believe in Jesus Christ, place our faith and trust in him, and accept what he has done for us. The promise of the Bible is that all who believe in Jesus Christ will be forgiven their sins. We appropriate this promise for ourselves through faith. Faith is how all the promises in the Bible are appropriated. We believe them and trust in the God who gives them to us. It is as simple as that!

What is hard about faith in Jesus Christ is that it requires humility on our part. Jesus described this kind of humility by saying that we must become like little children, open, willing, and trusting. There might be many reasons a person would not want to place their faith in Jesus. They might say, "Why did God chose this way and not another?" Or, "I worry about what God will require of me?" Or, "I would rather come to God on my own terms." We may have many reasons for our resistance; this is why it requires childlike faith. To come to Jesus requires that we let go of our objections in order to place ourselves into the hands of God. The good news is that Jesus has promised that he will not turn away anyone who comes to him. In fact he will give them eternal life, rest for their souls, and life that flows abundantly. This is the experience of those who give themselves to Christ in faith. He gives them new life that is richer and fuller than they could possibly have imagined.

For that reason, if you have never asked God to forgive your sins, why not take a moment to do so now. If you have never

56

personally placed your faith in Jesus Christ, why not take a moment to do so. Perhaps you have never really thought about doing this yourself, or never had the right opportunity. Here is your opportunity; don't let it pass. If you have never made your own personal commitment of faith in Jesus Christ, don't let this opportunity pass.

I would invite you to humbly pray a prayer like this, in your heart. "Dear God, I come to you with a humble heart and ask you to hear this prayer. I recognize that I am a sinner. I admit it. You know how far from your ways I sometimes have fallen. I believe however, that in Jesus Christ, you have promised to forgive me. I ask that you would forgive me for all my sins. I am truly sorry for them. Wash me clean on the inside and remove my guilt. Jesus Christ, I believe in you. Come live inside me. Make your home in my heart. Wash me clean and never ever leave me. Lead me and help me get to know you better. Thank you. I believe you hear this prayer. Thank you for forgiving my sins, receiving me into your family and kingdom, and for giving me eternal life in Jesus Christ. Thank you. Amen."

If you prayed that prayer and have never really prayed a prayer like that before, stop for a moment and thank God for allowing you to understand and receive his forgiveness. The scriptures say that Jesus stands at the door of our hearts and knocks. If anyone opens the door, he will come into them, and eat with them, and make himself known to them. That is the great promise of the Christian faith and that promise is for you. All who believe in Christ will be saved and that promise is now not just for everyone else, but for you as well! Thanks be to God!

PRAYERS OF INTERCESSION AND PETITION

We have mentioned three different types of prayer, so far, thanksgiving, praise, and confession. There are two more types of prayer we need to talk about. The next important kind of prayer is called *intercession*. This means praying for other people. This kind of prayer is one of the responsibilities of being part of the people of God. In Christ, we are brothers and sisters with one another. As such we ought to help one another and what better way to do so than to pray for each other? Sometimes the best thing we can do for another person is to pray for them.

Does God hear us when we pray for other people? The Bible says he does and this has been the experience of people throughout the history of the Church. Christians have prayed for the needs of others as if their prayers mattered and people of faith have constantly given witness to their belief that God's grace is present in their lives because others have prayed for them. We see examples of these kinds of prayers and the results that come from them throughout the Bible. The apostle Paul prayed for the churches he started and asked them to pray for him and his ministry (*Romans* 1:9, 15:30). He instructed Timothy to make sure the churches prayed for those in authority (*I Timothy* 2:24). Jesus encouraged us to pray, not just for our friends, but our enemies as well (*Matthew*

5:44). This is one of the basic things you will teach your child in terms of prayer: to consider others, to remember their needs, and to ask God to help them. These prayers are called prayers of intercession.

What about ourselves? Is it okay to pray for ourselves and our needs? There is a story about a woman who had gone to the pharmacy one day to get some medicine. When she got back to the car, she realized she had locked her keys in the car. She did not know what to do. Her husband was out of town. She did not have a spare key and had no one to call.

In desperation, she looked toward heaven and said a prayer, "God get me out of this mess. I need your help." When she opened her eyes, there was a motorcycle pulling up. It came into the spot right next to her. The driver got off. He was rough looking. Scruffy beard. Dirty clothes. He was a little scary, in fact. The woman, however must have looked distressed because he said, "Ma'am can I help you?" She told him her problem. He reached into his saddlebag and pulled out coat hanger. Within thirty seconds, he had the car door open.

She said, "O thank you sir. You are an angel God sent to help me." The man smiled and looked a little sheepish. He said, "Lady, I'm no angel, in fact, I just got out of prison yesterday for car theft." The woman thought for a moment, then looked to heaven. She said, "Thank you God, you are so good. You not only answered my prayer, you sent me a professional!"

Is it okay to pray for our selves and our needs? The answer of the Bible is, "Yes!" We may wonder if these are childish prayers,

59

but they are not. We know this because Jesus prayed for himself. In the Garden of Gethsemane, for example, he prayed about his upcoming suffering and asked for help and guidance. The Bible says that Jesus prayed at his baptism (*Luke* 3:21) when he certainly would have prayed for himself as the started his public ministry. If Jesus prayed for himself, then we can too. Our own needs should not be all we pray about; that would be selfish. We can also pray selfish and immature prayers for our wants and desires, that don't really have anything to do with God's plan for our lives. But Jesus did not discourage us to pray for ourselves. As another example, remember that in the Garden of Gethsemane, Jesus encouraged the disciples to pray that they would not enter into temptation. He also instructed us to pray for our necessities in The Lord's Prayer. It contains several prayers that are for our basic needs, like daily bread, help in temptation, and grace to forgive others. Jesus encouraged his disciples to look to God for their needs and requests. We call these kinds of prayers, *prayers of petition.*

The truth is, we never outgrow this basic kind of prayer. We never reach a place where we don't need to ask God for help. In fact some believe that petition is the essential form of prayer, because we are always like children in relation to our heavenly Father. We are God's children and we always need the grace and help our heavenly Father can supply. It is a sign of faith that we turn to God with our needs, not to other resources and not just our own wisdom. Instead of simply worrying or trying to do it all on our own, we bring to God our requests. Even if we occasionally pray a selfish or foolish prayer, God doesn't seem to mind. He just says, "No," and teaches us to pray more wisely.

What we have said in this chapter is that there are different kinds of prayer. All of them are appropriate at various times. We may not use them all every time we pray, but we should be sure to make praise, thanksgiving, confession, intercession and petition a regular part of our life of prayer.

PRAYING FOR YOUR CHILD

There is one thing we have not mentioned up to this point. It is that you, as a parent, ought to pray for your child or children. I once heard a grown adult say that his life went very smoothly until his mother passed away. Then all sorts of things didn't go nearly as well. The person said that it dawned on him one day that his mother had prayed for him every day and it was something that he and his life sorely missed.

Why is it important for you to pray? It is important for yourself, but there is another reason. It is important for your child. You want someone to pray for your child every day, but who will that person be? Who loves your child enough to pray for him or her every day? The answer is that you do. In fact, you are the person to whom God has given the responsibility, not only to raise your child but to pray for him or her every day. Perhaps no one else in the world will make the commitment to pray for them every day, but you will. You love them like no one else. You are committed to them like no one else.

You can and you must, pray for them. Only God knows how many things in their life depend on it.

So, add this to the other reasons you need to be a person of prayer. Your job as a parent is to pray for your child, every day, to ask God to keep them in his care, watch over them, guide them, help them in their decisions, and nurture their hearts toward him. You need to be a person who prays so you can pray for your child, because you want someone to bring them before God in prayer, every day.

One final thing to understand about prayer is that it is learned *by praying*. You don't learn to pray from reading a book or listening to a podcast. You learn by praying. You don't have to remember all we said in this chapter, though I hope it has been helpful. Don't wait until you have everything figured out. Start today and pray. Talk to God. Say thank you. Ask God for what you need. Pray for others. Tell him you're sorry for your mistakes. Praise him for his goodness. Do these things, not out of a sense of duty but to connect your heart and life with God.

We are going to continue to talk about prayer in the next chapter as there are a few more things we need to discuss before you begin to pray with your child. For now, however, try to turn your heart and spirit toward God when you pray. Know that God is listening and wants to commune with you in your prayers. When you pray, God comes near to listen in, makes his gentle presence felt, and draws close to you as you draw close to him.

4

UNDERSTAND THE NATURE AND PRACTICE OF PRAYER PART TWO

THE ONGOING PRACTICE OF PRAYER

IN THE LAST CHAPTER, we began to explore the meaning and practice of prayer. In this chapter, we will finish our overview of prayer. The purpose of doing this is to help you, as a parent, gain a higher comfort level with some general principles of prayer before you begin to teach your child how to pray.

We have talked, so far, about five basic types of prayer: Thanksgiving, Praise, Confession, Intercession and Petition. These are important to understand, but how do we actually learn how to pray? Did Jesus have any practices that teach us how to pray?

The first thing to understand is simply that Jesus prayed! Think about that. As close to the Father as Jesus was, he nevertheless made time to pray. A story in *Mark*, chapter 1, makes this clear. It is a story from the early ministry of Jesus. Jesus had spent the day teaching and healing people in a certain town. The people were amazed at the miracles Jesus was able to do. There was great joy in the village. Jesus' ministry had been a roaring success.

At the end of the day, Jesus must have been exhausted, emotionally and spiritually. If I had been Jesus, I would have put the "Do Not Disturb" sign on the door, pulled the pillow over my head, and not answered if anyone knocked. What did Jesus do? He woke up before dawn the next day and went out to find a quiet place to pray. Jesus here gives us an example to follow. If Jesus needed to pray, then we do too! If Jesus did not neglect the practice, then neither can we.

This leads us to a practice that has been used by Christians down through the centuries. It is the practice of developing a regular, devotional time for prayer. One of the things Christians have done through the centuries is try to organize their life so that they have a regular time to pray. This makes sense. If we are going to really know God and have a life with God, we must spend time with God, and what better way to do this than give time to our relationship with God on a regular basis.

People have sometimes called this the practice of a "Quiet Time," or a "Devotional Time." We make an "appointment" with God, so to speak, in which we spend time with God in prayer. This can be any time. It might be early in the morning before everyone

64

else is awake. It might be first thing when we arrive early at work before the workday begins. We might schedule our devotional time during lunch when we shut our office door, if this is allowed. It might be when the kids are taking a nap or when they head off to school. It might be at night just before we go to bed. Whatever the time and place, a classic Christian practice is to have a regular devotional time in which we turn our attention to the Bible and to prayer.

What is the best time of day for a devotional time? The best time is whatever is best for you. It will depend on your work and family schedule. It will also depend on whether you function best in the morning or the evening. In the beginning, you are looking to set aside 5-15 minutes every day to spend with God.

This is not something one ought to become legalistic about. You will sometimes miss your devotional time. Life gets in the way. But everyone ought to be able to be regular in this. Try to be consistent and faithful in making time for prayer. Former supermodel Kathy Ireland has developed a large licensing company, putting her name on all sorts of products for women. She is an incredibly busy and successful businesswoman. But she is also a Christian and has been since age 18. She is quoted in *Forbes* magazine as saying that her "first and last meeting every day is with God."[ii] If we want to live close to God, having a regular devotional life is one of the best ways to do so.

A good devotional time classically includes two things. One is reading the Bible. Christians read the Bible because it tells the story of God's work in the world. This means reading the Bible at home, not just hearing it read on Sunday mornings in church. One of the classic disciplines of the Christian life is to read the Bible at home.

This might be something you actually don't do. Lots of Christians have heard about reading the Bible and maybe thought about it but don't actually do it. They don't tell other people they don't do it, but they don't. It's why so many Christians don't know much about the Bible; they just haven't read it. If this is you, don't be embarrassed, just start reading it. Get a Bible. Make sure it is a newer translation; don't use your grandmother's Bible. The Bible quotations in this book are from the English Standard Version, sometimes called the ESV. This is a good, relatively new translation. The New International Version (NIV), New Revised Standard Version (NRSV), and New King James Version (NKJV) are also readable, modern translations. Get a Bible in a new translation that you think you will enjoy reading. Start in the New Testament, maybe in the gospel of *Mark*, and read a chapter or half a chapter, every evening before you go to bed or some other time during the day. You will actually get through a lot of the Bible over time this way and you will come to know what is in it. If you will do this, you won't be one of those Christians that has a Bible but never reads it!

Of course, reading the Bible might sound dull to someone who has never read it or only read it casually, but it isn't. The Bible has in it stories of love, betrayal, murder, sex, ambition, achievement, failure, jealousy, and family conflict. And, as author N.T. Wright has pointed out, we find all those just in the first book in the Bible, *Genesis*. Don't ever think the Bible is boring; it is anything but!

It is also never dull to read a book in which God might speak to you to give you guidance. When we pray we speak to God. When read Bible, God speaks to us. That is a simple but profound way to think about things. If you will read the Bible regularly, it will open up to you like a flower blooming in springtime. You will discover wonderful things in it that make you wise and bring you closer to God. In addition, reading the Bible is the perfect preparation for a time of prayer. It gives you things to pray about, cleanses your mind, and aligns your spirit with God. I cannot overstate the importance of reading the Bible! If you don't read it presently, start reading it. It will be one of the very best things you will ever do in your life and for your family.

METHODS FOR PRAYER

There are some good patterns you can use when you pray. One is the word Acts, like the book in the Bible. A-C-T-S. When you pray you might consider using this acronym. A – start with adoration, or praise as we have called it. Say prayers that praise God for his mercy and grace. C – next go to confession. Confess the faults and failings that come to mind. Be as specific as possible. T – Thanksgiving. Say thank you to God for his numerous blessings. Finally S – supplication. Pray for yourself and others. This is a good pattern to use in your prayers. A-C-T-S. Adoration, Confession, Thanksgiving, and Supplication.

Another helpful acronym is the word Pray, P-R-A-Y. First praise, P. Begin by praising God. Then repent, R. Confess your sins and repent of them. Then ask, A. Ask God for your needs and the needs of others. Finally yield, Y. Here is a type of prayer we have not mentioned. This is when we take a few moments to yield our heart, words, thoughts, and actions to God. This is another good pattern – P-R-A-Y, Praise, Repent, Ask, Yield.

Another helpful idea is simply to ask God what he wants you to pray for. I like doing this from time to time. Sit in the silence and listen to the thoughts that come to your heart and mind. Then begin to pray for those things that come to mind. Continue to ask God what to pray for then pray for things that come to mind, until you find your heart still and quiet, or you run out of time. Don't be too mystical about this and try to figure our what comes from your mind and what might be a nudge from God. Just pray about what seems to be on your heart and in your mind. This usually gives us plenty to pray about for a good time of prayer.

A good beginning plan for a devotional time is to read the Bible for five minutes then pray for five minutes. It is more important to strive for quality rather than quantity. You may eventually discover that your reading sometimes goes longer as well as your prayers. The issue is not how much time, however, but seeking to connect your heart and soul with the living God.

It is important to note that when we pray, we sometimes feel closer to God than at other times. Sometimes you may not feel much of anything. You read the Bible and say your prayers, and nothing much happens! At other times you feel a real sense of God's

68

presence. I would suggest you not worry about the times when you don't feel God all that much. On the other hand, don't get overexcited when you feel God very close. What I want to say is, don't focus on your feelings in prayer. Don't think that the success of your prayers depends on how you feel during any particular time of prayer. Even when you don't feel anything much, God is hearing your prayers. It is God on whom we ought to focus, not our feelings. But as we pray, over time, we will more and more often find ourselves aware of the gentle, peaceful, living presence of God when we pray.

An important aspect of prayer is to pray with faith. We see in the gospels that Jesus talked a great deal about faith. He seemed always to be talking about faith and encouraging faith. Why is that? It is because we appropriate the promises of God for ourselves through faith. All God's promises become real and true for us through faith. For example, God has promised to hear our prayers and answer them. This is a promise. So when we pray, we should believe that God is listening and ask God for what we need. Of course, he may not give us exactly what we ask for but will always give us something and typically he gives us what we need and better than we expected. So believe God is listening when you pray and know that he will reward you with his grace, his help, his guidance, and his answers.

Let's go back to a practical issue that has to do with prayer. Where should we have our devotional time? Is one place as good as another? We can pray anywhere of course, but in our devotional time, it usually helps to have a place that is conducive to being able to pray. Find a place where you can sit, read, and pray undisturbed. It will make praying easier. You may also discover that this quiet place becomes sacred over the weeks and months that you use it for your prayers.

In teaching your child to pray, you are going to help them create their own structured time for prayer just before they go to bed. You are going to create for them and with them a sacred space that will help them enter into the presence of God. Creating a place for prayer is going to be very important for your child and we will talk about how to help them do this in the next chapter.

OTHER ISSUES IN PRAYER

There is something else we learn from the example of Jesus. In addition to regular times of prayer, we see that Jesus prayed spontaneously. He would sometimes stop in the middle of an activity and voice a prayer to his heavenly Father. Sometimes he felt a particular need and said a prayer. On occasion, he felt grateful and stopped to give thanks. Sometimes he needed guidance and turned to prayer for strength and help. In the gospels, we have a number of instances of Jesus praying spontaneous prayers.

This is a second thing we learn from the life of Jesus. We ought to pray when the feeling strikes us, or when a moment of need arises, when a particular circumstance warrants, or when we feel especially grateful. Spontaneous prayers are quick and simple. "Lord, help me to keep my cool as I go into this meeting." "Dear

Lord, thank you for helping me avoid that accident." "Lord, help me know the right decision to make."

The good news is that God's Holy Spirit prompts us to pray, when we are walking along, when we are out in nature, or when our child does something that brings us joy. Sometimes, seemingly out of nowhere, we become aware of God and want to pray. Theologically, we say that this is God's Holy Spirit within us, nudging us, reminding us of his presence, drawing us to himself, and inviting us into prayer. Be grateful for these moments and respond to them. God wants you to pray and for this reason reminds you of his grace. Listen for God's nudges and be aware that he is with you as you go through your day. Another thing we learn from the example of Jesus is that he gave special attention to praying in times of decision, temptation, and crisis. When we examine the life of Jesus, we see that he was tempted, got tired, felt hungry, had moments of rejection as well as success, was loved by some but hated by others, and finally experienced betrayal and death. Jesus lived life in all its ups and downs, just like we do. In his moments of crisis and decision, he gave special attention to prayer. For example, he prayed at his baptism and just before his temptation. He prayed all night before he chose the 12 apostles. That must have been a difficult decision and he spent time talking with his Heavenly Father about it. Jesus prayed in the Garden of Gethsemane before his arrest as he faced the reality of the cross. On the cross, in the midst of his sufferings, Jesus prayed. He even died praying, saying, "Father, into your hands I commit my spirit." This reminds us that when we find problems facing us, or decisions to be made, we ought to make time to pray.

There is a wonderful story told by Truett Cathy, founder of Chick-fil-A, in his book titled, *Eat Mor Chikin: Inspire More People*. He talks about a major decision concerning the company in its early years. As he thought about the decision, he didn't want to make it alone but with the family and with God. He got the family together, including the children, for a family discussion. They discussed, then prayed. Only then did they make their decision. As it turned out it was the right decision and would have far-reaching benefits for the future of the business.[iii] The Bible says that God gives grace to the humble. If we want God's help and guidance, we should spend time in prayer and trust that God will guide us.

You will sometimes experience the problem of concentration in prayer. How do we keep a thousand thoughts from running through our heads, when we are trying to pray? The truth is, sometimes we sit down to pray and we can't cut off the noise in our mind. The worries of the day and the things on our to-do list just won't go away. We have been so busy during the day that we can't just "turn it all off." This kind of inner noise makes prayer difficult. It is one reason morning is a good time to pray, before our minds get too crowded. Someone has noted that as it is better to tune your instrument *before* you play rather than afterwards, it is good to pray before the responsibilities and challenges of our day. One thing you might do to help with concentration is to pray in the morning before all the mental noise gets started. Set your quiet time first thing in the morning, especially if you function well in the mornings or get up

72

before everyone else. If you cannot have a long devotional time in the morning, at least turn your first thoughts to God as you wake up. Use this still and quiet time, first thing in the morning, to lift your spirit to God, if just for a few moments.

It is also good to realize that most people can't immediately get into the mood to pray. We have to calm ourselves down a bit. Settle in. Let go of some of the worries of the day for a while. One good practice is to take a minute at the beginning of our prayers to calm our mind, heart, and spirit. Close your eyes and be still. Gather yourself. Collect your spirit. After about a minute you will find yourself calmer and more ready to pray than if you just jump into things.

Reading the Bible or a good Christian book also helps prime the pump to get us into the mood to pray. In addition, when unwanted thoughts come up, just let them come. If they remind you of things you need to do, write them on a piece of paper to deal with later. Since these are what you are thinking about, use these as the first matters for which you pray. Pray about whatever is on your mind. At some point, you will begin to be able to let go of these things and experience a release of your heart and emotions to God.

HEARING GOD

One question people ask is how do we hear God in prayer? We said that prayer is like having a conversation with a friend. This is true, except that God is invisible and doesn't speak to us in an audible voice. It would be nice if we heard God speaking in an audible voice, but he doesn't. For this reason, the issue of "hearing God" becomes problematic.

Think about it this way. Every child has to learn language. Learning language doesn't happen overnight. It takes time, years in fact. Eventually, however, the child learns what words mean. They learn to *hear* what is being said. Like a child learning language, we have to learn the language of how God speaks to us. We have to come to discern God's voice. It usually comes in those little nudges in our heart that lead us toward what is good. It usually comes very gently, almost imperceptibly. God nudges us toward the right ways. God may speak through other people or through circumstances as well, but don't be impatient with this process; over time you will learn to recognize God's nudges and leadings.

Sometimes, of course, we mistake God's voice or mishear. We ought to test what we think we hear, to be sure it is God's leading not just our own wishes or things that come out of our own mind or something we want to hear God say. Over time, we will begin to get a sense of God's guidance, what is God's voice and what isn't. Of course, one of the ways God speaks to us is through the Bible. When we read the Bible regularly, verses will come alive for us and give us help for our daily life. This is the work of the Holy Spirit who is at work in you to make Christ come alive in you and to lead you into his ways.

Prayer is multi-faceted and it is the way we live in relationship with God. Underlying all the things we do in prayer is one overarching purpose, communion with God. If you love someone,

74

what do you want to do? You want to spend time with them! That is what prayer enables us to do with God, spend time with him. It also enables God to spend time with us, where he has our attention.

Something also happens within us when we pray. Have you ever noticed that if you spend enough time with another person, you begin to take on certain of their characteristics, even little phrases and mannerisms? It is eerie how this happens and is one of the reasons we ought to keep good company. When we spend time with God, what happens? Something of God rubs off on us. We are subtly changed. Our hearts are softened. Our attitudes adjusted. Our tempers calmed. When we commune with God we come away with something of the heavenly presence of God imprinted upon our heart and soul.

The great purpose of prayer is communion with God. Only God can calm our restless spirits, fill the empty void inside us, and help us find our true selves. Though we often try to fill the void with other things, only God truly satisfies. When we connect with God, we discover a depth of peace, meaning, and stability for our lives that nothing else provides.

Pass Your Faith To Your Children

5

FINDING A TIME AND PLACE

WHAT IS THE BEST TIME?

IN THIS CHAPTER and the next, we get to the simple method you are going to use to pass your faith along to your child. This simple method is to teach your child to pray, at bedtime, and for you to pray with him or her. The heart of this approach is to teach your child to pray their own real and authentic prayers, saying thank you to God and asking God for what they need. In teaching them this simple practice, you will bring them into their own relationship with the living God. We will talk later about why this works so well and why this is so important, but in this lesson and the next, we are going to teach you how to teach your child to pray in a simple but profound and life-changing way.

The simple practice of praying with your child may not seem particularly profound. Can this simple practice make a big impact? Does it have the potential to bring a real and living faith into the heart of your child? The answer is, "Yes." This simple practice has extraordinary impact and value. You will see why as we go along. Be patient for the present. Laying a solid foundation is important, so that you, as a parent, understand exactly what you are trying to achieve and how to accomplish it. What you are aiming for is your child to come into their own authentic, personal relationship with God. You are going to discover that this is easier than you think through the simple practice of praying with your child. Please do not think that the simplicity of this approach is an indication of its significance. What you are going to do with your child will change their life forever, in positive ways you cannot imagine or foresee.

So where do we start in teaching our child to pray their own authentic prayers? There are three simple but key aspects to this. We will look at them in order. The first is finding a time and place. The second is giving your child a simple method. The third and final one is, of course, having your child actually pray. So let's start with the first of these, finding a time and place.

I need to mention something that we have not addressed up to this point. It is that you are going to teach your child to pray *out loud.* You may not have thought about this detail. You may have just assumed that your child would be praying silent prayers, but I am going to suggest that a key ingredient for teaching them to pray well is for them to pray out loud, with you. If they will learn to pray out loud, they will also be able to pray silently, but it is better to start *out loud* rather than silently. You also will pray out loud with them. I will tell you why later in this lesson, but I want you to know where we are going before we start talking about choosing a time to pray, because when we look for a good time, we are looking for a time when you and your child can say a simple prayer *out loud* together. We are going to make this very comfortable, both for you and your child.

The first thing we need to do is find a good time to pray with our child that gives us the time, privacy, and opportunity to pray with them. There are several possibilities here. I know people who pray with their children when they are sitting in the car line waiting to drop them off for school. I know people who hold hands in the kitchen and pray before they walk out the door to school. You may choose from a number of possibilities, but I want to suggest a time that I think has numerous advantages. You may choose a different option and you can still use these principles to make it work, but I would invite you to seriously consider the method I am going to suggest, because it has a number of advantages that will both help ingrain the habit of prayer into your child's life, and help you grow in your relationship to them.

How do we start in teaching our child how to pray? The best answer is to start at bedtime. For parents to say bedtime prayers with their children is a time-honored practice, but I want to recommend a practice that is different from what has often been done.

Saying prayers at bedtime is not something new. For many generations, parents taught their children the simple prayer: "Now I lay me down to sleep; I pray the Lord my soul to keep. And if I die before I wake, I pray the Lord my soul to take." This 18th century prayer was the way children learned to pray for many generations and obviously not without some measure of success. More recently the last part of the prayer has become something like: "Guard me Lord, throughout the night and wake me with the morning light." With either version, it has been an effort by parents to instruct their children in the practice of prayer. I remember kneeling beside the bed at night when I was young, and saying this prayer with my mother. I learned something from doing so, though I also remember it made my knees hurt. There is a better way than using this prayer however. There is a way to take your child much further in the practice and experience of prayer than simply helping them learn this children's prayer or one like it. While memorized prayers have their place, there is a better way to start.

What parents of previous generations got right, however, is that bedtime is a wonderful moment in which to teach the practice of prayer. It may be the *perfect* time, for a number of reasons, as we will see later. Most people who pray, generally say a prayer before they go to sleep. They may fall asleep in the middle of their prayers, but they at least start them at bedtime, if they do not always finish them. This is more than just a cultural practice. Nighttime is a *natural moment* that is perfectly suited for the practice of prayer. The Bible talks about it as a good time to pray and to teach your child to pray.

When the book of *Deuteronomy* instructed parents to teach their children, it indicated some appropriate times when this teaching should be done. One of them was at bedtime. *Deuteronomy* says, "You shall teach them to your children, talking of them when you are sitting in your house, and when you are walking by the way, and *when you lie down*, and when you rise." (*Deuteronomy* 11:19,

80

emphasis added). What were they to teach? God's laws! Notice that this verse mentions, "when you lie down," as a good moment to teach God's commands to our children. The Old Testament then, saw the moment just before the child fell asleep as an opportune moment for instruction in God's laws. It is also a wonderful moment to instill the habit of prayer.

David, the writer of many of the psalms, spent long nights awake protecting the sheep, when he was a shepherd. As he wrote psalms, he remembered his nighttime prayers as special moments of communion with God. In Psalm 63, he said, "My soul will be satisfied as with fat and rich food, and my mouth will praise you with joyful lips when I remember you *upon my bed*, and meditate on you *in the watches of the night*" (Psalm 63:5,6 emphasis added).

We can obviously pray at any time and we have already noted how morning is a good time to pray, before our minds get crowded with the problems of the day. But in terms of teaching your child to pray, there is no better time to start than with a prayer at bedtime just before your child goes to sleep. What I am going to suggest is that you take 5 to 10 minutes with your child right before they go to sleep. You will use this brief time to be with your child and instill in your child the habit of prayer. This is a biblical time that is appropriate for both praying and teaching your child about God. It is a practical time that makes it easy on you and your child. It will also develop in your child a lifelong habit of closing their day with God. If your children are between ages 4 and 12, it is particularly easy to use bedtime as a time to teach them to pray. In this chapter, I am thinking primarily about children who are 12 and younger. We will talk about teenagers in chapter eight.

BEDTIME AND YOUR CHILD

Every family has their own bedtime routine. Some parents are laissez faire about bedtime; it happens when it happens. Other parents are the bedtime police, with rules that vary little from day to day, and citations given for failure to comply. Some parents allow their child to go to sleep in their room, the parents' room, or even to sleep with them. Your child may go to sleep on the couch and then you carry them to their room after they are fast asleep. Some parents like the total anarchy approach and let their child choose their own bedtime, which, when they are young, is a practice destined to make both you and your child irritable in the morning. Most parents, however, have some sort of regular bedtime for their child, at least on school nights. If you do, it will make it relatively easy to teach your child to pray. If you do not, you will need to consider how to create a bedtime routine. It will not only help your child get a good night's sleep but will work to your great advantage in teaching them to pray.

What makes bedtime difficult is that children generally do not want to go to sleep. Remember when you were a child? You wanted to stay up as late as Mommy and Daddy. You wanted to watch one more episode of the television show, or at least until the next commercial. And then you wanted to stay up until the *next* commercial. Children don't want to go to bed. But here is a place where you need to be the parent. That your child has some sort of regular bedtime is very important, because you will use this time to sit with them for a few moments, have relaxed conversation with them, and teach them to pray.

The truth is that bedtimes are important because children need a lot of sleep. They are growing both physically and mentally. It is during the nighttime that their minds and bodies renew their energy for another day of learning and growth. You as an adult might be able to function with just a few hours of sleep. You have learned to function when you are not at your best and you can have a cup of coffee the next day, or three or four cups. But children need a solid night's sleep. When we started to get bad behavior from one of our children, we would say, "When you start acting like this, we think it's because you didn't get enough sleep last night. So tonight you're going to bed early." It served the purpose of discipline and was often true. They were just tired and having a hard time controlling their behavior. A good night's sleep made for a new child the next morning. For the sake of your child, it is best to have an appropriate bedtime and, for the most part, stick to it.

Children sometimes have trouble going to sleep. For this reason parents may let them stay up until they are more tired, and sometimes until they are literally exhausted. But going to sleep is a learned skill. Just as a child can learn to speak and say, "Thank you," and add 2 plus 2, they can learn how to go to sleep. I remember one night when our oldest child was young and wanted me to lie in the bed with him until he fell asleep. I had done this with him from time to time. He enjoyed it and, quite frankly, I did too. But I soon realized that once I started, there was no end in sight. One night, he said, "Daddy, will you lie down with me until I go to sleep?" I was tired and ready to spend some time with my wife. I replied, "No, Robert, you are old enough to go to sleep by yourself." He thought for a moment, then replied, "But Daddy, I'm only three!" I felt awful, but had already made the decision not to lie down with him. I replied, "You're still old enough to go to sleep by yourself."

Of course, that is exactly what he did. He went to sleep! I tell that story to acknowledge how easy it is to get into bad habits where bedtime is concerned. This is where it is good to remember who is the parent and what is in the child's best interest. One of the things that builds self esteem in children is learning to do new things. One of the achievements of growing up is learning to go to sleep by yourself. We deprive our child of the good feeling that comes from mastering this skill if we pamper them too much. We also disrupt a perfect opportunity to teach our child to pray.

It is also true that having a bedtime for your child is important for you as an adult. Most of us need some "wind down time" after a hard day of work or at home managing the family. We need to have some moments to relax before we go to sleep. Personally, I can't just turn the day off and immediately go to sleep, unless it's Sunday afternoon and a football game is on and I'm in the recliner. Then, it's pretty much lights out! But on a normal evening, I need some time to wind down. Your child's bedtime is important because you need some time to watch TV, or read a book, or talk to your spouse, or straighten up the living room, whatever helps you wind down. You need to put your child to bed so you can have some time for yourself, your marriage, and things you like to do or need to do.

When your child comes into the world, it is easy to think of them as the center of the family. In the beginning, they certainly demand an inordinate amount of time, energy, and effort. But they are not the center of the family, even though it feels that way. The two people who started the family are the center. These two people are you and your spouse. Without you, this child would not have come into existence. If you are married, the very best thing you can do for your child is to stay together with your spouse. That is why you need to give attention to your marriage as well as your child. In the first years of your child's life, this is especially difficult, because children require a great deal of attention. But remember who started it all. You did! Keep your marriage healthy and you do your child a huge favor.

In addition, putting your child to bed, so you can have some time to yourself or with your spouse is one way of sending the message to your child that they are *not* the center of the universe. You have some priorities that do not include them. You are a better parent, if you have some things to think about, work on, and do besides center your life around your child. A regular bedtime for your child helps you do this and it helps your child as well. It is good for your child to understand that life does not revolve around them.

I say all this not primarily as an advocate for bedtimes but because bedtime is the perfect moment to turn your child's attention

85

toward God. It is such an ideal time that anything you have to do to make it possible will be worth the effort. If at all possible then, set a bedtime for your child that is appropriate and be consistent with it. And here is the key. Don't make it so late that you or they feel the need for them to go to sleep immediately. Make their bedtime such that there are about ten minutes for you to sit with them. This is the time you will use to teach them to pray.

PRAYING OUT LOUD

In this process, I am going to encourage you to do something that may seem counterintuitive, pray out loud with your child. For some people, praying out loud with their child will come easily. For others this will be more challenging. If the idea of praying out loud makes you nervous, let's talk about it briefly. The average person would rather go to the dentist than pray out loud, no offense to dentists. Or lead a field trip of 5-year-olds to the zoo. They say that the two greatest fears people have are speaking in public and praying in public. But this is not exactly praying *in public;* it's just praying in front of your child. And they are only five! So, relax; we are going to make this easy for you and for your child. Before you know it, the experience of hearing your child pray aloud will be one of the joys of your life and you won't be self-conscious about your prayers either.

You might ask if it might be better, or at least just as good, to pray silently. But who does that make more comfortable, your child or you? I suspect you. Silent prayer is important, but there are several reasons it is better for you both to pray out loud, in this setting. First, it is the way you monitor what your child is praying. Your child will understand some things about prayer instinctively, such as the need to be grateful and that there is a God who hears their prayers. But other things will need to be taught to them. For example, when it comes to praying for things, they will need some instruction. The only way you can "coach" them in their praying is to hear what they say. I did not personally worry about correcting every little misstep in my child's prayers. When they prayed for their toy, or for the house, or that a certain team win the ball game, I did not immediately jump in to correct them. Some of this they will grow out of as they grow up. What I did was gently coach them to the kinds of things for which we ought to pray. I said, "Normally, we do not pray for our house, we thank God for our house. We pray for people and not objects." I would often wait until the next evening so it did not feel like a correction but a piece of instruction. I might also say, "Normally you do not pray for your team to win. People on the other team might be praying that they will win. It is usually better to pray that everyone will play hard and play their best and that no one will get hurt."

These small coaching tips are important. Through them you gently guide your child in the practice of prayer. It is one of the important reasons for them to pray out loud; otherwise you will not be able to correct their misconceptions about God and about prayer.

There is an important by-product of the practice of praying out loud with your child. In this process, you will have many opportunities to teach them about God. For example, when you correct your child's misconceptions about prayer, you are also teaching them about who God is and how God interacts with them and the world. This is one of the great things about what you are going to do. In teaching them about prayer, you are really teaching them about God, helping them understand who God is, what God is like, and how they should relate to God. In the course of talking to them about prayer and answering their various questions about God (which we will discuss in chapters nine and ten), you have the opportunity to help them rightly understand the person, character, and will of God. This will be invaluable to them because you will help them develop an authentic understanding of who God is and how he wants us to respond to him. The good thing is that you will be able to do this in your various conversations with them at bedtime in a way that is not awkward, forced, or uncomfortable. In teaching them to pray, you are also teaching them about God and in doing so, you are fulfilling one of your God-given responsibilities as a Christian parent, to teach the Christian faith to your child. Teaching your child to pray is the perfect vehicle to allow you to impart a right understanding of the Christian faith to your child.

MODELING PRAYER FOR YOUR CHILD

Another reason for you and your child to pray out loud is for them to hear *you* pray. One of the ways they will learn to pray is by hearing you pray. They cannot do this if you do not pray out loud.

But when they hear you pray, they learn how it is to be done. They also learn the proper respect and attitude they ought to bring to their praying.

If you have not prayed out loud very much in your life, you may have questions. For example, what tone should you use? I would suggest casual but reverent. You are modeling for your child the attitude to bring to one's prayers. Make your prayers casual, meaning do not use a lot of "Thee's" and "Thou's." Pray in your normal voice and do not try to take on a religious "voice." Don't say, "Gauwd", in some affected or "super-holy" way, just say, "God." Pray normally and informally. This teaches them that God is approachable. The goal is not prayers that sound a certain way but prayers from the heart. Be reverent but casual and this will teach your child to do so as well.

Once you start this process, your child will expect you to pray out loud with them. If you are asking them to pray, they will expect you to do so also. This makes sense if you think about it. If prayer is important, and it is, then they need to see that it is important for you. If you expect them to pray, they will want to know that you pray also. If they think that you don't pray, then they will assume this is something only children do and they can stop when they get to be an adult. That is not the case, of course. You are teaching them a practice they will do for the rest of their lives, so you need to model this for them. If you show them that you pray and you think it important it will give credibility to the practice in their eyes. Of course, if prayer is good enough for them it must be good enough for you. If they need to do it, and they do, then you do too.

You might be worrying, at this point, if you pray well enough to pray with your child. You may feel like your prayers might not set a good example for your child. I would not worry about this. If you don't think yourself very profound or polished, your child will not notice. After all you are teaching them. They assume you know more than they do and the fact is that you do. Use the same pattern they use and learn to pray yourself. If you have never prayed much or not prayed much out loud, here is your opportunity to learn. Take advantage of it. You do not have to be light years ahead of them when it comes to praying; you just have to be one step ahead. With what you have learned so far, and what is to come, that will not be difficult. So don't worry and don't apologize. Don't say, "Well, I'm not very good at this, but here goes." Pray with confidence. Even if you feel some inadequacies, don't let them show.

When you pray with your child, you also do not need to bare your soul or be more honest than is appropriate. Your time of prayer with your child is not your primary time of prayer. You should have your own time for prayer when you bare your heart to God, bring God your petitions, and pray for things God places on your heart. When you pray with your child, you need to pray in ways that will seem appropriate to them. For example, if you have had an argument with your spouse that day, don't pray, "Dear God, let mommy and daddy get along better." That will make your child anxious and send them to bed worrying. Save that for your own time of prayer. Just pray for everyone in your family, as you typically do, and let it go at that. Don't over share in your prayers with your child. As you have taught your child to say prayers of thanksgiving
90

and prayers of petition, you should be able to find appropriate things for which to thank God and appropriate things for which to pray. Say prayers with your child that are honest, make sense to your child, and are not so personal as to make them uncomfortable.

I said just a moment ago that in teaching your child to pray, you are going to teach them about God. This is very important and gives you a unique opportunity. In this practice, you are going to sit with your child beside the bed and pray with them at night. You are going to teach them to close their eyes and do two things, say thank you for their blessings and ask God for things they need. What are you teaching them about God in this? You are teaching them, first of all, that there is a God. You are affirming God's existence to them. You are telling them that you believe there is a God who loves them and will hear their prayers. This is a basic but crucial thing for them to know and understand. When they get to be adults, it will be this basic issue on which their lives will turn. If they believe in God, they will turn toward him in faith. If they do not, then they will live their lives on their own and without God. In praying with your child every night, you are affirming one of the most important things they can know; there is a God who cares about them and who listens when they pray.

There is a wonderful verse in scripture that affirms this truth. It comes from the book of *Hebrews*, chapter 11, verse 6. It says, "And without faith it is impossible to please him, for whoever would draw near to him must believe that he exists and that he rewards those who seek him." That verse lays the foundation for and gives us the basic promise about prayer. Prayer is based on the belief that God exists and that it is worth our effort to seek him. This is the foundation of prayer and this is what you teach your child when you pray with him or her at night. There is a God who is good, who loves us, who listens when we pray, and who rewards those who seek him.

The Bible says throughout that God does reward those who seek him. This is true for you and it is true for your child. If your child will pray, God will listen and God will reward them. He will reward them with his presence, his grace, his help, and his kindness. God will make himself real to them in ways you don't foresee and in ways beyond your ability to teach. He will make himself known to them because they are entering into a real relationship with the living God and it is not a one-way relationship. God will do his part in the relationship; he will reveal himself to your child. He will meet them in unexpected moments. He will speak to their heart and life and call them toward himself. In teaching your child to pray, you do the best thing you can do for your child, which is to bring them into relationship with the God who will watch over them, guide them, and be with them all their lives. That is what you are doing when you teach your child to pray and this is why it is so important.

We have focused in this chapter on a practical time for teaching your child to pray. If you already have a regular bedtime routine with your child, then you are ready to go. If you don't, see what you can do to arrange your schedule to create a time for prayer, right before your child goes to sleep. This is the time you will use to teach your child to pray. In the next chapter, we get down to the nuts and bolts of how to start your child into their own life of prayer.

92

6

GET STARTED WITH YOUR CHILD

A SIMPLE BEGINNING

WE NOW GET DOWN to the practical details of teaching your child to pray. You will discover that this is a very simple practice and one that makes sense. It is also going to be completely natural and not make you or your child uncomfortable. Praying with your child may be something you have thought about doing or even done occasionally. But the benefit of teaching your child to pray does not come from doing it occasionally but regularly over an extended period of time. In addition, your child does not benefit from it if you *think about* doing it but never actually do. As I have already said, the value and impact of this simple practice cannot be overstated. While this seems simple and perhaps only minimally important, it will be of huge significance in your child's spiritual development. Do not underestimate the value of what you are about to do!

Implementing this practice may take some courage on your part, especially if you are slightly uncomfortable with praying aloud, but I hope you will not be overly anxious. Nothing about this practice should be awkward. Nothing will be unnatural. Everything will be simple if you will follow the guidance of this chapter. You will also discover that beginning the practice of prayer with your child will fill your heart, as a parent, with joy and satisfaction. Do not be afraid; you are about to enter into a wonderful journey with God and with your child. It will be one of the best things you will ever do in your life!

Here then is the heart of this method. There are two simple things to teach your child about praying in the beginning. The first is to teach them to say, "Thank you" to God. The second is to teach them to ask God for things they need. These two kinds of prayer will serve them well for the upcoming years and indeed for the rest of their lives. This is where you are going to start. Someone has suggested that most prayers are either "Thank you, thank you, thank you," "Please, please, please," or "I'm sorry, I'm sorry, I'm sorry." You are going to teach your child to say "Thank you" to God for God's blessings and to ask "Please" for things they need. We will talk about prayers of confession that say, "I'm sorry," in a later chapter.

Considering Some Details

The heart of this method is to sit with your child in their bedroom at night, just before they go to bed, and pray with them. This ten-minute period, right before they go to sleep, is the perfect time to teach them to pray. Where should you sit? Sitting on the bed is a nice way to order this time. If this is not convenient, find a chair that you can pull beside the bed. Pull the covers up on your child. Tuck them in. Every child likes to be tucked in. Then sit on the bed or beside the bed. I would also suggest that you turn the lights down. It is easier for your child to pray with the lights low rather than with them shining in their eyes. It is also easier to tune out other thoughts with the lights low.

You want your child to be comfortable for this time of prayer. For most children, that is not kneeling to say their prayers. They might get used to kneeling, but it would take a while. In my experience kneeling guarantees a short prayer. You want your child to be able to pray as long as they want without becoming uncomfortable and quitting. I would suggest that they lie down in bed, ready to go to sleep. Have them lie down in bed, on their back looking up at you, as they do when they are going sleep. This is a good position from which they can pray.

You are doing two things here. You are getting your child ready to go to sleep, but you are also creating a space and a mood that will be conducive to both conversation and prayer. What will happen in this setting is that over time it will become a sacred space. Without being too mystical about it, some places become sacred for us because God meets us there. My hope is that your child's bedroom at night will become one of these sacred places, though they may not realize it for many years. Their bedroom at night will become a place where they regularly sense the gentle presence of God. Turn off the overhead light, dim the lamp, tuck your child into bed, and, in the few minutes before they go to sleep, help them turn their heart to God.

When should you start this practice? It is never too early to begin doing things to nurture the spiritual dimension of your child's life. There are lots of simple but effective things you can do to encourage faith in your child when they are very young, like taking them to church, telling them God loves them, reading them simple Bible stories (from a book with a lot of pictures), and singing religious songs with them (or using a musical book, if like me you don't have much of a singing voice). In the first four years, these are very good ways to lay a foundation of faith and belief, and our children loved doing these things. Use your parental role here to teach some first understandings about God. Children are wonderfully trusting. If you tell them God loves them, they will believe you. Of course, you are telling them the truth and it is a truth that will sustain them their entire lives, if they will hold on to it.

But when should we begin to teach them to pray? We began the practice that I am describing in this chapter when our children were age four or five. You can't really sit on the side of their bed while they are still in their crib and maybe not even when they are in a "day bed" that is a transition between a crib and a real bed. We began the practice shortly after they got into a real bed. It was shortly after our youngest child got into their own single bed that we began the practice of teaching our children to pray. Up to this point we read them Bible stories, took them to church, and occasionally said a prayer with them before we put them to bed. When they get into their own bed, however, it is the perfect time to begin to teach them to pray.

PRAYERS OF THANKSGIVING

How do we start the practice of teaching our child to pray? The key is not to overcomplicate things when you introduce the idea to your child. Tuck them in, dim the lights, and sit on the side of the bed. Then simply say, "We are going to start saying our prayers at night and here is how we are going to do it." You may get some initial resistance. Even a child who already is growing in their understanding of God may not initially receive the practice with open arms. It is new and they do not know what they are getting into. Do not worry. Gently tell them what is going to happen and start. You do not really need to work into it. Say something like: "We are going to start saying our prayers at night. I am going to say a prayer then you will say one. I want you to say something you are thankful for." Start with one simple thing. Have them say something for which they are thankful. In a week or so, you can add the second part, which is teaching them to pray for their needs and for other people.

You have to teach them how to open and close their prayer. As a pastor, I often instruct people about how to pray out loud. Here is what I say and this is essentially what you are going to tell your child. I tell people, "When you pray, you need an opening and a closing and you need to say something in the middle. It's as simple as that." When you pray, you need to have an opening. It can be something like, "Dear God," or "Our heavenly Father," or "Gracious Lord." Prayer opens by addressing God; when people pray out loud, they usually use a standard opening like one of these. When teaching our children to pray, we used the phrase, "Dear God."

Your child will also need to know how to close their prayer. Christians generally close with, "In Christ's name, Amen." Or you can just say, "Amen." It is probably easier for you to teach them simply to say, "Amen," when they are finished. The heart of prayer is what you say in the middle, between the opening and the closing. Generally people do two simple things, they thank God for blessings then ask God for what they need. If you listen to people pray aloud, you will hear these elements. There is an opening and a closing. What is said in the middle tends to be prayers of thanksgiving and prayers of petition.

What you are going to do is teach your child to open their prayers by addressing God, say a prayer in the middle, then close by saying, "Amen." It is as simple as that; so don't overcomplicate it. When I began to teach my children to pray, I said, "Let's open by saying, 'Dear God'. When you are finished, say, 'Amen.' In the middle, tell God something you are thankful for." After this simple instruction, I modeled what this might be like. I prayed a short
98

prayer, like, "Dear God, I thank you for a pretty day today and that we always have enough of food to eat. Amen." Then I said, "Now you say, 'Dear God' and say something you are thankful for. Then say, 'Amen.'" Then you simply let them have a shot at it. Wait and let them say their prayer. The first few nights all you want them to do is say thank you to God for one or two things.

They might balk and say, "I don't know what to say?" If that happens, coach them. Say, "Well, what are some things you are thankful for?" Let them tell you what they are thankful for. They might say, "Well, I'm thankful for my friends, and my toys, and my family, and my dog." You reply, "Great! Pick one or a couple of those and tell God you are thankful for them." Then you tell them to start with "Dear God" and say their prayer. Tell them to say, "Amen," when they are finished. Start small and simple. Importantly, don't let them off the hook.

This is the heart of the method you are going to use to teach your child to pray. This may seem simple or even simplistic, but do not underestimate the importance of this simple practice. You will see, as we move along, how profoundly the experience of praying at night will impact your child.

When beginning this practice, it is important not to let your child off the hook. Tell them what to do, model it for them, then wait. Be quiet and see what happens. What will happen is, they will pray. They will pray a simple prayer but one that is real. That is how children are. They do not have much pretense to them. If they just pray one short prayer and thank God for one thing the first night, you are on your way. All you have to help them do the first night is thank God for one thing.

PRAYERS OF PETITION

Once you introduce prayers of thanksgiving, continue in this way for a week or so. Have your child say a prayer for several things they are thankful for each night. In this beginning stage you are hoping they will thank God for more than a couple of things. You want them to begin to think of a number of things for which they are thankful and include them in their prayers. Let that come naturally. When you are satisfied that they are getting the concept of prayers of thanksgiving, then introduce the aspect of praying for themselves and other people. This is a little harder for children to grasp, because it takes some abstract thinking, but with a little coaching, they will get the picture quickly.

A week or two after you begin this process, say something like, "Now we are going to start including prayers for ourselves and other people. After you have told God a couple things you are thankful for, pray for something you want God's help with or someone who needs God's help. You might pray about something you are concerned about. You might pray that you have a good night's sleep. Or you might pray that your grandmother feels better and gets over her cold. Or you might pray for a friend at school. Or for all children who do not have enough food to eat." Do not give them too many options, just some they can latch onto. Then, let them go for it. Be quiet and let them pray. If they stumble, help them. If it gets quiet when they get to the part about praying for someone, give them a prompt. Say, "why don't you say, 'help grandmother to get well.'" They will follow your prompt and say their prayer. In doing so they will enter into the larger world of praying for other people. It is a responsibility and privilege they will have all their lives, because a responsibility of life as a Christian is to pray for others. As long as they live and pray, they will continue to make praying for other people an aspect of their prayers, and you will have taught them to do so! How about that!

Every night, as they say their prayers, you will need to pray too. In the beginning, you should pray first. The first few nights, you begin and show them what you want them to do. This models for them what you are asking them to do. As we said, start with a simple prayer of thanksgiving. "Dear God, I thank you for my family and my friends. Amen." Do not pray a fancy prayer or a long one but one that is simple. This way your child knows that they don't have to pray a fancy prayer either. Model for them what you want them to do. Then eventually add prayers for yourself and for others to your prayers. "Dear God, thank you for a beautiful day and plenty of food to eat. Help all the children around the world that do not have enough food to eat. Amen."

It is *very* important that you pray *out loud* with them and begin by praying first. I eventually changed the order so that our child prayed first, then I prayed. They may want to do this soon, so they don't have to wait for you to get through, and this is fine. In fact you want them to pray first after they get used to praying, so they don't

101

fall asleep while you are saying your prayer. For the first few times, you go first, to model what you want them to do. They will get the hang of this very quickly, then you can switch the order so they go first.

Let me repeat that it is very important for you to pray out loud with them. They learn not only by praying but by hearing you pray. This is why it is very important for you to pray out loud. The truth is, you need to pray, just as they do. You need to thank God for things, ask God for what you need, and pray for others. You will, hopefully, have your own devotional time of prayer, but it will not hurt you to pray with them. We all need prayer and this is another opportunity for you to pray.

You may feel your inadequacies about prayer arise at this point, but don't be anxious. You can do this; in fact you *must* do it. You are the very best person to teach your child how to pray. *You must do this with your child!* The beauty of this is that y*ou* as their parent are going to teach your child to pray. What a wonderful legacy! Not only is this the biblical way children should learn about the faith, but they will always thank you for it. Years from now they will be able to tell others that they learned to pray from their parents. It will be a legacy of your love for them that they will be able, in turn, to pass on to their children. As you are doing for them, you are teaching them to do for their children. For that reason, you are not only impacting the lives of your children but your grandchildren, and great grandchildren as well.

A NOTE TO FATHERS

We need to say something to fathers at this point. In recent decades women have often overshadowed men in the life of the church. For a number of reasons, women have responded to the gospel with more ease and greater enthusiasm than men. Women are blessed with a tender and open heart that the gospel easily penetrates. Men sometimes are just a bit more stubborn! Men need adventure and challenge; the church has not always provided it. The church, without knowing it or meaning to, has preached a soft gospel that did not speak to the needs of men. If you, as a man, have found the church less than stimulating, you are not alone. But in the beginning it was not so. Remember that Jesus' twelve apostles were all men. They certainly did not find Jesus dull or uninteresting. In fact they found his message revolutionary. They found it so compelling that they left their homes and livelihoods to follow Jesus around the countryside. They would be the heart and center of an early church that would change its world in just a few centuries.

The absence of men in the spiritual training of their children is a major problem in the church today. From the perspective of the Bible, fathers are crucially important in the spiritual nurture of their children. The Bible teaches this throughout. In the scriptures, it is fathers who are supposed to take the lead in training their children, teaching them the faith, and raising them in the training and instruction of the Lord. While mothers do an admirable job and are equally important, when fathers neglect their God-given responsibilities, the family suffers significantly.

As a man, your father may not have taken on a role of spiritual leadership in your household when you were growing up. For that reason, you may not have a good role model in this regard. You may not have experienced your father as being active in your religious training other than perhaps taking you to church. The reason may be that his father did not take part in *his* religious training, so it was difficult for him to know exactly what to do. Because of this, you may not realize the vital role fathers can and need to have in the religious nurture of their children.

All of this is to say that you, as a father, need to be involved in the practice of teaching your child to pray. In fact I would encourage you to take a leading role. *You* take the lead in making this happen. *You* be the one to start this process. *You* be consistent with your child in praying with them before they go to bed. This is especially important if you have a boy. If you do not pray with your son, he will get the subtle message that faith is not something for men, at least once they grow into being a man. But if you, as his father, will be a role model that he knows prays and who prays with him, the practice will be credible in his eyes.

This is no less important if you have a girl. If you want your daughter to grow up and marry a person with faith, you have to show her your faith. She is going to want to marry someone like her father. Show her that being a man means having a deep faith in God! What better gift can you give your daughter than to show her that a man should not only be strong and brave, but humble before God!

If you are married, you will have to work out the details of how you both participate in this process. You will have to decide who puts them to bed each night and who says their prayers. My strong encouragement to fathers is that you at least split this time with your wife. Be an equal partner with her at the very least. If your wife has spent much of the day with the children, it is a perfect way to give her some time off. You as the father, put them to bed, and say their prayers with them. It will give your wife a break and give you some quality time with your child. What you will discover, as a bonus, is that this becomes one of the most delightful moments of your day. It will become one of the most intimate and important parts of your interaction with your child.

GET STARTED

We now have a time, bedtime. We have a place, in the bedroom, with your child in bed and you sitting beside the bed. We have a method, each prays out loud, saying what they are thankful for, then asking God for their needs and the needs of others. The last thing to do is, get started. *Just get started!* Think through your plan and start. When you tuck your child in, tell your child you are going to start saying prayers at night. Tell them how to open and how to close. Tell them to start by saying one or two things for which they are thankful. After a week of doing this, teach them to pray for themselves and others. You go first, so they can hear what it sounds like. Then have them pray. Coach them as needed. After a week change the order and have them go first. That is how to begin. Do this and you are off and running.

The important thing to understand is that this really works and it will start working the night you begin. It will start slowly, but you will be amazed at how soon you will hear unrehearsed, untaught prayers flowing from your child's heart and spirit. Before long you will hear your child thank God for things and pray for things you never imagined to hear them say. You will discover that they have an inborn ability to believe in God and reach up to God. In short you will discover that your child is *really praying*. They are not going through the motions. They are not faking it. They are not just trying to please you. *They are praying!* How about that! They are addressing God as if it were the most natural thing in the world to do. Of course, it is! While we as adults lose track of this reality, our children bring fresh hearts to the practice of praying. They sense and know that they are doing something right and good and true.

A crucial thing to understand is that, once you begin this practice, you should do it *every night.* This is not nearly as effective if only done sporadically. Model a faithful commitment to prayer for your child by being consistent. Unless there was some emergency we would *never* go to bed without saying our prayers. On occasion, if our child was exhausted, after I had tucked them in, I would say, "Let me say a short prayer for us tonight." One way to signal the importance of prayer to your child is to make it something you do together *every night,* not just a couple of times a week. You don't need to be legalistic about this, simply consistent. It became such a
106

habit in our kids' lives that they could not go to sleep without it. Let me repeat this! If you will do this every evening, it will become such a part of your child's routine, that they will help you be consistent about it. They won't be able to go to sleep without it. They will want this time with you and with God and this is exactly what you would like to see happen. For that reason, show your faith by doing this with your child every evening. This helps them become confident in the fact that God is listening and that bringing their prayers to him is important.

One of the bonuses of this practice is that it gives you a wonderful opportunity to have a private conversation with your child, about all sorts of things, not just God. We discovered that the child who would not talk to us during the day, would suddenly become quite talkative at night. In part, they just didn't want to go to bed yet, but still, they were talking to us. It is an intimate time between you and your child that both you and your child need. This will become one of the most intimate and meaningful moments of the day, both for you and for your child.

What is happening in this process is that, through the act of praying, your child is aligning his or her life with God. They are turning their heart toward God once every day, right before they go to sleep. It will be the last thing they do at night. Hopefully, at some point, God will be someone they think about as soon as they wake up. You are starting them in a practice that will help them, throughout their lives, order their lives by God's purposes. They are developing practices that will enable them to survive tough times, because they know they are not alone; God is with them. What is happening is that they begin, even at an early age, to tap into the resources of the living God. Remember that Jesus said, "Let the little children come to me and do not turn them away, for of such is the kingdom of heaven." You will realize how true those words are when you see how willingly and honestly your child opens their heart and life to God.

What is happening is that they are turning their lives toward God, and *God is responding*. I cannot overstate this last reality. What is happening when they pray is not a gimmick. It is not just a psychological feeling. It is not just a mood created by a dark room. What will happen is that God's Holy Spirit will begin to make his home in their hearts. Remember that Jesus said that where two or three were gathered in his name, he would be there in the midst of them. When you and your child pray, the promise of Jesus is that he will be present. Jesus is in your midst! By the power of the Holy Spirit, Jesus comes to listen in. He comes to make himself known. He comes to reveal himself both to you and your child.

This does not mean that you should expect lightning bolts from God. If that happened it would certainly terrify you both. No, the moving of the Spirit of God is gentle, almost imperceptible. What happens, however, is that over a period of time, as you pray, you simple *feel* like God is there, listening in. It is not something you can put your finger on. It just feels right. It feels like God is near. There is peace and calmness in your spirit. *You* feel this and here is the thing, *your child will feel it too*. Though he or she will not be able to articulate it, they will begin to know that when they pray it *feels like* God is present with his calming Spirit, listening to their

108

prayers. This is the presence of the Holy Spirit. In teaching them to pray, you are ushering them into the presence of the Holy Spirit. Of all the things you will ever give them in their lives or do for them, this is the most important. It is certainly the most enduring, because it has eternal consequences.

You now have what you need to get started. Do not be afraid. Step out in faith and trust that God will help you. He will and you will be surprised how easy this is. Though it may seem simple, what you are doing will change your child's life forever. Not only will it give them a foundation on which to build their life; it will connect them with the living God, whose promise of salvation and eternal life is for all who believe. In teaching your child to pray, you are helping them put their faith in the living God. There is no greater gift you can give them as their parent.

God's blessings on your first steps. Let me close us in a prayer that models this method. Let's open with a simple phrase, "Dear God." Let's close by saying, "Amen." In the middle, let's say a couple of things we are thankful for then pray for a couple of things.

"Dear God. Thank you for this day, full of your mercy. Thank you for the opportunity to impact my child's earthly life and eternal destiny by teaching my child to pray. You know that I love my children dearly. I know you love them too and want to make yourself known to them, just as you have to me. Help me have courage and wisdom, as I begin this process with them. Help me overcome my anxieties and fears, so I can impact my child's life for good. Lord, I commit this effort to you. Be with me. Bless me and more importantly bless my children in this process. I love you very much. Amen."

7

MAKING PRAYER A HABIT
WITH YOUR CHILD

GROWING IN PRAYER

IN THIS CHAPTER, we want to talk about some potential problems you might face. However, as I said before, if you start this practice with your children when they are young, it will go very smoothly. The most important thing is to start them in the practice of prayer and be consistent in it. The matter of consistency is very important. Pray with them every night. This makes their relationship with God something they consistently nurture and not something about which they only occasionally think.

To address some practical issues, what do you do if you have more than one child? The answer depends on whether your children sleep in the same bedroom. If they sleep in the same bedroom you may want them to say their prayers together, especially if their bedtimes are the same or close together. If their bedtimes are the same the answer is simple; have them say their prayers together. They each say a prayer then you say yours. You may want to alternate which of them goes first or just get into a pattern with which they are comfortable. If they sleep in the same room, but their bedtimes are not exactly the same, you may have the opportunity to pray with one while the other is brushing their teeth. Then the other one comes in and you pray with that child as the first is falling asleep.

My wife and I have two children who slept in different bedrooms growing up. Because they were two years apart, they had slightly different bedtimes. I said the prayer with the youngest first, then went to the room of the oldest. It worked out fine. They had a 15-minute difference in their bedtimes; this gave me 15 minutes with each child to talk and say their prayers. It usually did not take this long, but it gave a window of time for each of them.

Even if your children have their own bedrooms and say their prayers separately, there should be some times when they say their prayers together, just for the experience of doing so. We let this happen naturally. When we went on vacation, for example, they often slept in the same bed or bedroom. We have two boys and this is how it worked for us. On those occasions, when it was time for bed, I turned off the lights and sat on the side of the bed. After we talked about the day for a few minutes, I said, "Okay, let's say our prayers. Who wants to start?" They both said a prayer after which I said one, and that was that. My wife and I thought the experience of praying together important for them. They needed to hear each other pray. They needed to be comfortable praying with one another and

112

other people. When they are old and I am long gone, I want them to be able to pray with one another with some comfort, though they may not have many occasions to do so. In our family, I have wanted prayer to be something we can do together without embarrassment. Having them pray together on occasion has been one way we have tried to develop this ability.

It is probably good for you to have an individual time of prayer with each child most of the time, if possible. Even if several children sleep in the same bedroom, each child having their own personal prayer time is ideal, if it can be arranged. The reason is that this gives you individual time with your child. This is quality one-on-one time that you may not get with them any other time during the day. The same is true for them. Just before they go to bed every evening, they know they will have your undivided attention. They know they will have their own personal time with you, without the distraction of chores, homework, siblings, or other interruptions. This is a time when you as the parent, can look into their eyes and let them know, through your presence and attention, that they are supremely important to you.

In today's fast paced and hectic world, even our children need some time without any agenda or schedule. They need some "face time" with the people around whom their world revolves. Without much restructuring of your family routine, this brief time of prayer and conversation gives you quality time with them that few things will be able to match. *Do not let anything steal this time from you and your child!*

I once heard a former NFL football player talking about raising his son. He expressed the importance of parents being present in their children's lives. He said, "When I am present at my children's activities, it lets them know they are important. In fact it affirms their existence." I found that comment striking. For a parent to be present for their children "affirms their existence." I have thought about that comment over the years and I believe it is true. When a child's parent is not there for them, it creates a deep wound in their soul. A child thinks, "If my own parent doesn't love me, then who will? I must not be very loveable." That is why saying prayers with your child at night gives you a unique opportunity to nurture their spirit. When you take the time to pray with your child at night, it speaks to their heart and soul in ways beyond what you realize. You let them know, by your presence, that they are supremely important. They are worth your time. They are of value in your eyes. In doing this you represent God to them. By letting them know that they are important to you, you signal to them that God thinks they are important also. That you love them is the foundation for their growing belief that there is a God who loves them very much.

FOR WHAT SHOULD WE PRAY?

Your children are going to pray some silly and selfish prayers at times. Children have a limited view of the world and limited concerns. What should we do when they pray not to have to go to school tomorrow, or when they pray for their room? Depending on their age, the answer is, "nothing," at least at first. At first, especially if they are young, do not do anything. You are glad they are praying. They are praying about things that are important to them. They are praying from the heart; that is what you are after. Get them praying and let this become a habit. Then you can adjust their praying along the way.

Are there things for which for which we should not pray? There is an old baseball story about Gil Hodges and Yogi Berra. I do not know if this is apocryphal or not, but I love the story. Yogi Berra was catching and Gil Hodges came up to bat. Hodges made the sign of the cross with his bat in the dirt. Yogi said, "Gil, what are you doing?" Hodges said, "I'm saying a prayer that I will get a hit." Yogi replied, "Gil, why don't you leave God out of this and just let him enjoy the game!"

We have all said prayers about getting a hit, passing an exam, doing well on our presentation, and so forth. Are those wrong? No. Sometimes God answers those prayers in wonderful ways. When that happens it encourages us about the reality of God and the value of prayer. The Bible seems to be more concerned with people not praying at all or not praying with consistency, than with them praying a few inappropriate or selfish prayers.

There is not a list of things *not* to pray for in the Bible. Our common sense gives us some guidance, however. In general, we do not pray for wealth to use on ourselves, things that merely promote our self-interest, and things that might not be in the interests of others. Again, the scriptures do not seem overly concerned with things not to pray for. Sometimes God even answers our selfish

115

prayers, as an encouragement to us. The real problem, much more than that people pray for the wrong things, is that people do not pray at all. God helps us over time discern the difference between good prayers and bad ones by which ones get answered. Our inappropriate prayers generally do not get answered. Our appropriate ones do much more often. Use your common sense and what you know about the general direction of the Bible and you will do fine in guiding your child's prayers.

Think about things for which your child ought to pray. They ought to pray for their family. They ought to pray for their friends. These may get repetitious from time to time and that will ebb and flow. I would not worry too much about this. They may pray every night not to have bad dreams and that is fine. That's what they are worried about so that's what they should pray for. On occasion, you can encourage your child to keep their prayers fresh. I sometimes said, "Don't just say the same thing tonight. Include some new things in your prayer." This encourages them to think creatively. It encourages them to think in a wider way about the world and their life. In addition, because the circumstances of your child's life will continue to change, they will always have something new to pray about. For each of us, life presents new challenges, so there is always something about which we need to pray. Isn't God good in that he continues to give us new material for our prayers!

RESISTANCE

You should expect some resistance from time to time in the practice of prayer. This is normal. We all resist the grace of God; this is human nature. This resistance may come out in the form of, "Why do we have to say our prayers?" Or, "Can you say them for me tonight?" Or, "Do we have to say our prayers *every* night?" If you start your children early in the practice of prayer, you will not have much of this. Prayer will just be what you and they do. But you will occasionally get some resistance. On those occasions, gently but firmly tell them that everyone is going to say their prayers, so they might as well get on with it.

To the comment, "Can you say the prayer for me tonight?" I usually respond in one of two ways. Sometimes, especially when they are tired, I will say a prayer for us both. There is no reason to be rigid about things. You are not after performance of a duty. You want them to pray from their hearts. Sometimes they really *are* tired. Sometimes *I* am tired. On occasion it may be easier for one person to say the prayer and everyone get to bed. On occasion I may say, "I said the prayer last time, tonight you say the prayer for both of us."

Under normal circumstances however, I will not let them get away with not saying their prayers. I might say, "If you are tired, say a short prayer. But you still need to say your prayers." Then I simply say, "So you start." If they complain, I might say, "You are just taking up your time. It would be faster to go ahead and pray." On occasion I will remind them of the theological principle, which is that everyone has to say their own prayers; no one can pray for them! They have to do their own praying! Since that will be true their entire lives, it is true now. They need to say their own prayers!

One thing we did was encourage them to make prayer part of their daily life. When they had a test coming up, I said, "When it comes time for the test, relax, say a prayer that God will help you think clearly, then do your best." This was a simple reminder to pray about things going on during their day. You will be surprised when your child will actually do this. They will take you at your word and say a prayer before their test. It will become a part of their learning how to include God in their daily lives.

Be patient with this process of praying with your child and let it evolve over time. If you start your child in this practice early, you will pray with them every night for ten or fifteen years. The regular aspect of this practice over a number of years is part of its power. For that reason, you will have time to incrementally teach them about prayer and add various elements to their prayers over time. Be patient with the process. Take it one step at a time. Let their faith grow naturally and don't try to rush it. Like an acorn growing slowing into an oak, they will slowly but steadily grow in their faith into young Christian disciples. Delightfully, you will be able to watch it as it happens.

There is an unanticipated benefit that comes from praying with your child and having your child pray out loud with you at night. The benefit is that your child gets practice praying out loud in front of others. This turns out to be a very useful skill and one they will have opportunity to use as they grow up and get involved in the

118

church as an adult. Most people are terrified of praying in public. As a pastor, I have gotten used to doing it, but it was not always comfortable for me either. When I first became a pastor, I suddenly got asked to say the blessings at the family reunions. My mother used to say to me beforehand, "If you get asked to say the blessing, sound like a preacher." I never did quite figure out what she meant. I think she meant don't make it too short, but no one else seemed to mind. I have gotten used to praying in public because I have gotten a lot of practice doing it, but most people do not have many opportunities to practice. For that reason, they go into panic mode if they are unexpectedly asked to pray in front of others. Perhaps they wonder if they need to sound like a preacher?

There is a secret to praying in public, however. It is to do exactly what you have been teaching your child to do. You have to open; you have to close; and you have to say something in the middle. Usually people say the two types of things you are teaching your child. They thank God for something, then ask for something.

Think about the value of what you are teaching your child. Though they may not realize it, you are giving them the skills to be able to pray out loud in front of other. In addition, they are getting practice in doing so. These are skills that will turn out to be very useful one day. When they suddenly get called on to pray, maybe at the family reunion, they will know what to do. Open. Thank God for some things, like the chance to have all the family together and share good food. Then pray for something, like a good time of fellowship and safe travels home. Then close. It really is not more complicated than that.

One of the reasons people sometimes hesitate to get involved in church is that they are afraid they will get called on to pray. Because of this fear, they stand on the sidelines. Many people who would be great leaders in the church never allow their gifts to be used because of this private fear. Praying in front of others is not difficult, however, if you use the pattern you are teaching your child.

To give an example, imagine that you are in a church Christian Education Committee meeting one evening and the chairperson unexpectedly calls on you to pray. What do you do? First, open. "Dear God." Then thank God for something appropriate for the setting. "Thank you for our church, for our educational program, and for the opportunity to work together tonight." Then pray for something. "Help us to be productive and wise in our decisions. Especially bless the children and youth in our program so that they will grow in their faith." Then close. "In Christ's name, we pray. Amen." It is as simple as that. Use this pattern and you can pray excellent prayers, even when asked to do so unexpectedly.

PRAYER AND DISCIPLINE

One issue that every parent has to deal with is discipline. Discipline is very important, not only for you as a parent, but for your child. What is the point of discipline? It is to teach your child to behave; that is the classic answer! As my parents said to me on occasion, "Children should be seen and not heard, so when we go out, I don't want to hear anything from you." They said this when we were going somewhere and they expected my sister and me to be quiet and not make a scene!

It is true that children need to learn the appropriate behavior for various situations and parents should help them know what is expected. There are certain behaviors that are appropriate for the grocery store, a neighbor's house, the soccer field, and church. Children need to be able to distinguish between various settings and know how to act in each. I remember my parents often telling me beforehand where we were going and what was expected. Even when I didn't like it, I knew what I was supposed to do.

Parents also need to discipline their children for the sake of the family. When children run wild in the household it is not good for anyone, including you as the parent and other siblings. As the parents, you have the right to establish discipline in your home for the sake of peace and order in the home. No one benefits from chaos.

There is another, often overlooked reason, to discipline your children effectively. It is that external discipline helps children learn internal discipline. This is very important for parents to understand. In disciplining your children, you are not just teaching them good manners but self-control. That you do not allow your child to have ice cream at four o'clock in the afternoon helps them control their appetite and their urges. That they can't make a scene in the grocery store helps them manage their behavior internally and control their conduct. That they can't run freely throughout the church hallways on Sunday teaches them to respect the needs of others, even when it goes against what they want to do. When children have external

121

discipline, it helps them learn to control their urges internally and this is crucially important.

You can think about discipline as a cone that is wide at one end and small at the other. The small part of the cone represents your child's younger years. These are the years to discipline them strictly and keep the boundaries tight around them. Help them know right from wrong. Teach them to control their behaviors. Don't let them talk back to you. Or hit their sibling or you. Don't let them act out or cop an attitude. Be hard on them early because they really don't know how to behave. Your job is to teach them how to behave and help them develop good attitudes about things. If they have to sit still and eat their dinner with manners, it helps them learn to appreciate and value the food in front of them, unless it's spinach, of course; some battles you can't win.

If you will discipline your children strictly when they are young, then as they get older, you can ease up. This is what the wider part of the cone represents. Once your children have learned to behave and control their impulses, they can be given more leeway, because they have learned to manage themselves.

The problem comes when parents reverse the cone. If you are permissive with your child early, they will not develop internal disciplines. When they get to be teens, you will realize your mistake and try to crack down on them. At that point, however, it is much more difficult. When they are young, you will get compliance, if you are patient and consistent in your discipline. Once they become teens however, you are much more likely to get rebellion. Discipline is relatively easy when children are young but much more difficult when older. Use the window of opportunity God has given you and help your child develop their own inner discipline and self-control. By doing this, you save yourself a lot of headaches and you do your child a big favor.

How do discipline issues impact your time of prayer with your child? One of the things I always tried to do was not to take out my frustration with my child in our time of prayer. That is, if I was upset or angry with them for some reason, I tried not to let it bleed over into our prayer time. If I had to punish them that day, I tried to resolve it by bedtime. Then I let it go and everyone moved on. To do this, of course, you have to be able to resolve discipline issues in your family. As a parent you have to find appropriate methods of discipline that fit a particular act of bad behavior, selfish attitude, or disobedience. But if at all possible, administer any punishment before bedtime so it does not color your time of prayer.

On occasion, at night, I might mention something that happened during the day. This quiet time may be the perfect time to give closure to something that happened. I sometimes said, "Do you know why Daddy punished you earlier?" Then I waited for the answer. If they understood then it was over and done. I simply said, "See if you can do better next time." If they did not understand why they were punished, I explained it again, so the lesson stuck. If there was a behavior that I did not like, but did not punish, I might say, "Do you know what Daddy did not like about your behavior at the dinner table tonight?" Then we had a conversation about it. While I had their undivided attention I tried to make the point that needed to be made. Then we moved on. I tried not to belabor the point unless absolutely necessary. Your time with your child at bedtime is the time for prayer. Use another time for correcting behavior, when at all possible. After whatever conversation we have needed to have, I simply said, "Okay, let's say our prayers. You go first." Again, bedtime is the time in which you both need to connect with God in prayer. But it can be a time to deal with issues of behavior or attitude if used sparingly.

One more thing. Your child may need to squirm, from time to time. When they do something wrong, don't immediately fix it for them. They need to experience some remorse on occasion. They need to feel guilty when it is appropriate; this helps them develop a sensitive conscience. It helps them know the feeling of guilt and not like the feeling. It helps them avoid doing wrong because they know how terrible the guilt will feel. That is not a bad thing.

8

PRAYING WITH TEENAGERS AND OTHER CHALLENGES

THE CHALLENGE OF THE TEENAGE YEARS

THERE IS GOOD NEWS for parents who start this process with their children when they are young. When your children reach their teen years, they will have a foundation in God that will be invaluable. It does not mean they will not have their struggles and challenges. Nor does it mean you will not find parenting difficult at times. It does mean, however, that you have a much greater chance of their navigating this time successfully than if they had no foundation in God. Because God has come into their lives as children, he will not leave then as teens. The authentic relationship with God they have begun will remain with them as they move into adulthood. If you will start the process of teaching your child to pray

125

between the ages of four and twelve, it will make your experience of parenting a teenager much smoother than it otherwise would be.

The challenge of the teenage years is that your relationship with your child is changing. An obvious transition is taking place. You have guided them by your authority up to this point. You have told them what they had to do, and they have had to do it. But your child now is on their way to becoming an adult. At this point, you begin to guide them, not just by your authority but through your example and influence. As we said in the last chapter, the dilemma with the teenage years is that if you clamp down on them too tightly, you will get resentment and rebellion. You have to guide them but with a lighter touch. You become less able to push them; you are going to have to pull them along with you by the quality of your relationship with them. They are going to do the right they less because you are making them do it. You want them to do the right thing because they know, inside, that it is the right thing to do and because of their relationship with you. In addition, if you have been teaching them about God and teaching them good lessons when they were young, those things do not go away. They may get inundated, at times, by a flood of hormones and other crazy things that are going on, but those lessons are still there; you just need to keep reminding your child of them.

This does not mean that you lose your right, as a parent, to set boundaries for your teen's behavior. There are times when you still have to say, "I love you and because I love you, you can't go to that party," or stay out late at night, or whatever they want to do that you don't think good for them. But this instruction has to be in the

126

context of a relationship with them that is authentic, supportive, and positive.

What do we do when our children become teenagers in terms of praying with them? Do we still try to sit on the side of their bed? Do we still go in and pray with them like when they were five? The basic answer is, yes, if you can! You may or may not sit on the side of the bed with them, but if you can, you still want to go in and pray with your teen, if at all possible. You still use the same principles. You need to be close to your teenager and this gives you a perfect opportunity. If you can sit on the side of the bed, do it. Though they are bigger in stature they still need physical closeness with you. They still need your affirming touch, pats on the shoulder, and physical connection with you.

One of the things we have discovered is that the issue of bedtimes become more complicated when a child becomes a teenager. Teens begin to want to set their own bedtimes and most of them will stay up later. They may resist a set bedtime and this can make a time of prayer harder. They may have homework to do that keeps them up later than you stay up as the parent. Unless they are staying up very late, however, which they don't need to do except on rare occasions, there is usually some time before they turn out the lights for them to say their prayers. Do whatever you can to pray with them as many nights as possible.

You are trying to make sure that the practice of prayer does not disappear from your child's life. Prayer is for people of all ages. There is never a time in their lives when they don't need to pray. Remind them of this. We do not ever grow out of the need to pray,

127

no matter how old we are. They need to keep their connection with God strong, now more than ever. Prayer is something people of all ages need to do. They are no exception because they have become a teenager. They are not suddenly a privileged person that is too good for prayer! Even though they are growing up, they still need to pray!

Your teen might say something like, "I don't really need you to say my prayers with me any longer. I can do it myself." A good reply might be, "I know, but I really enjoy it and it gives us some time together. If it's okay I want us to keep doing this together." Your teenager may not talk to you as freely as they did when they were young. At least they may not do so as often. That is the way teenagers are. But the fact that they know they have your undivided attention once every day, gives them the opportunity to talk if they want to take advantage of it. They may not do so as often, but sometimes they will. Pull up a chair beside their bed and have a seat. Or sit down with them wherever they are; they can stop their homework or video game or reading for a moment. By doing this, you continue to be a reminder to them about the importance of keeping God in their life by praying every day. And it gives you some one-on-one time with your child that you may not get any other time during the day.

Be creative in finding ways to nurture the spiritual life of your teen. I know a family with two teenagers that stops what they are doing at ten o'clock every evening. They gather in the living room for a family prayer. Each person prays out loud. Then they can either go to bed or back to their homework if need be.

Your teenager may not always act like they need a close connection with you, but they do. They may act like they don't want you around or in their space. They certainly do not need you in the same ways that they needed you when they were young. Your child is becoming an adult and they can do many more things on their own. But they still need you even when they act like they don't. You are still their parent. You are still one of the people who loves them more than life and has their best interests at heart. Down inside they know this, though they may not always show it.

If you start praying with your child at an early age, I would suggest that you change whatever parts of your routine necessary to help them keep prayer a part of their life on a regular basis as a teen. If you start when they are young, don't stop when they get to be teenagers. Just keep right on going as much as you are able, but do so with a light touch. Use your influence more than your authority. If they have been praying with you since an early age, they will have become accustomed to the practice of prayer. They may be able to pray as well without you; you hope this is the case. But do whatever is within your ability to keep them praying and keep their relationship with God authentic and fresh.

STARTING THE PROCESS WITH A TEENAGER

What if you did not start the process when your child was young? How do you start it with a teenager? As we have said, this process is very easy when your children are young, incredibly natural and easy. So if you have young children, please don't wait to start teaching them to pray. Start them young and it will give them a great foundation with God. But if your child is already a teenager, it is not too late. It may be more difficult, but there is still time. However many years you have with them in the house, whether 6 or 4 or even 2, you still have time to teach them to pray and help them connect their lives with God.

I would suggest that you start in a way similar to how you would start with a younger child, though you may need to do more explanation. You also might need to be more honest about why you are starting the practice. You might say something like, "I have just realized that we should have been praying at night since you were young. I need to have been teaching you how to pray. But I don't think it is too late, so I want us to start to pray together at night. This is not something I am going to just ask you to do. I will do it too. It will be good for you and good for me. We are going to start with a simple prayer and then go from there. How does this sound?"

You will probably have to field some questions. "I don't really need to do this." I would respond, "Actually, yes you do and so do I." Or they may say, "I know how to pray, but I like doing it on my own." You can respond, "Good. I'm glad you know how to pray. That will make this easy. But everyone can learn how to pray better and we are going to learn to do so together." They might respond, "Why all of a sudden? Where does this come from?" You can say something like, "It may seem sudden, but we should have been doing this for a long time. That is my fault. But I can't let you leave this house and head to college without prayer being a regular part of your life."

You know your child and you probably have a feeling for how much resistance you will get. One way to deal with this might be a family meeting. Family meetings from time to time can be a helpful way to talk about things going on and let everyone have a say. They are also a good way to gain some "buy in" from your child or children. To have a family discussion does not mean that the family suddenly becomes a democracy. You as parents still have the deciding vote. But it can give your children a chance to have some ownership in the decisions that are made. The more ownership they have, the easier it is for you to get compliance.

You might have a family meeting and say, "One of the things we should have been doing is teaching you to pray. We should have started this earlier, and that is our fault. But it is never too late to do the right thing, so we want to start saying prayers with you every night. So let's have some conversation about how to do this in the best way." Then you open up a conversation about what you want to do, and when is the best time to do it. As a family you may decide that the best way is to have a family prayer time at 10 p.m., or 9 p.m. or some other time. If your teen has some input into this, they will be more likely not to grumble when it comes to actually doing so. You may work out the details of how to do this at night with them alone. There ought to be some time you can go to where they are, either in their room or where they are doing their homework, for a brief time of prayer together. The goal is openness and buy-in from your teen. As the parent be flexible. If you give a little, they

131

generally will too. What you want to get from this is a time in which you can pray with them. Be flexible on minor details if it helps you secure this time.

If you get resistance, you might appeal to their sense of fairness. "We do a lot for you. This is one simple thing we want to ask you to do for us." You also might appeal to their love and respect for you. "This is really important to us. I would really appreciate it if you would do this with us." By this time your child may have an evening reading routine. They may like to read for 15 or 20 minutes in bed or they may like to listen to music to wind down. There is no reason that should interfere. Whenever you go in, they can stop their reading or listening to music for a few moments. You can say your prayers together then they can pick up where they left off. When lights out time comes they can turn off the light and go to sleep.

I have a friend who remembers what his father used to say to him and his siblings when they came to visit. This applied to when they came home from college and when they came to visit as adults. His saying was, "If you take shelter under my roof on Saturday night, you will go to church with me on Sunday morning." The reality is that, as the parent, you have the right to make some demands. There are some expectations that come with being part of your family. It is fair to ask your children to walk with you in the journey of prayer. You are providing food, shelter, and many other things for them. You have nurtured them in their lives and provided for their needs. They are not visitors in your home; they are members whose sustenance and livelihood depends on your assistance. It is fair to expect that they will respond to some of your needs. One of those is to teach them to pray. If they only see it as humoring your need in the beginning, that is okay. In time they will come to see the value, because God will meet them in the act of praying.

HUSBANDS, WIVES, AND SINGLE PARENTS

We have talked in a number of places in this series about both husbands and wives as part of this process of teaching children to pray. Today not every family fits into this pattern and many families do not have both parents living in the same house. This means that you might be sharing custody with an ex-spouse or have custody of the children on an every other weekend basis. You might be raising your children with a step-parent or be a step-parent yourself.

If you are the only parent in the home, what you need to do is straightforward; you take the responsibility of engaging in this process with your child. If you are on good terms with your child's other parent, it might be possible for you both to use this method. That would be a very good scenario. If your ex-spouse does not want to be part of this process, however, you can use it when your child is with you and it will make an impact. Teach your child to pray and do so with confidence. Your ex-spouse will, most likely, not interfere. You may be tired at the end of a workday yourself, but you will still find this time renewing and refreshing. It will be a great time of relationship with your child that you will both value.

If you are raising a step-child, you can also use this method, especially if the children are young. It may be that the biological parent ought to take the lead in this, but it isn't necessary. Use your judgment and talk it over with your spouse. If you are not the biological parent, and it is okay with your spouse, it might be a great opportunity for you to bond with your step-child, in a meaningful way. Use your good judgment; be wise but determined. Do what needs to be done to introduce your child, or your step-child to the living God by the simple act of teaching them to pray. This is not a matter of small consequence but of the greatest importance. In teaching your child or step-child to pray, you are saving their lives, both in this life and the one to come. Do everything within your power to help them come into relationship with the living God, through the act of developing their own authentic life of prayer.

There is another reality that I observe as a pastor; it is that husbands and wives are often not on the same page where spiritual matters are concerned. One spouse wants to go to church; the other one does not. One spouse cares deeply about spiritual things; the other is lukewarm or disinterested. Even in families where both parents have a religious faith and commitment, there can be a variety of opinions about spiritual matters.

The answer in general is that you always work with what you have. If you are the spouse who has energy for spiritual things, then that is the place to start. It is great when both parents are on the same page; the reinforcement of both parents being committed to serving God is a very significant positive example. If possible, both of you should be involved in nurturing the spiritual life of your child and what I said about fathers in chapter six still holds true. If the father will be involved in this process, it will give the practice a crucially important degree of credibility and impact. It serves as a role model for boys as to what it means to be a man. For girls it gives them a model for the kind of man they want to marry when they grow up.

Of course, one of the primary things you can do for your child is love your spouse. If you love your spouse, you create a stable environment in which your children can grow up. If your child's family life is stable, they can go to school with confidence to learn and without anxiety about their home life.

What if your spouse does not want to participate in this practice? The good thing about this method is that one parent can engage in this process at bedtime all by themselves. Your child may ask, "Why doesn't Daddy ever say prayers with me?" You might respond, "This is just something you and I do." Or "Your Daddy prays in his own way." Notice that neither of these are completely satisfactory responses. They leave questions for your child to deal with, such as, "Does Daddy not believe in God?" A better response might be, "That is a good question. Why don't you ask Daddy that?" There is nothing wrong with putting your spouse on the spot a bit, if you think it appropriate. You also might say to your spouse, "Our son asked why you don't ever say the prayers with him." If he or she is open, it might be the opportunity for them to become involved in the process. This way it is not you asking your spouse to participate in praying with your child; it is your child asking. Let your spouse join you in the nighttime prayers as a way of knowing what to do, then let them take their turn when they feel ready.

You always want both of you involved if at all possible. While one person may be the primary person who puts the children to bed, to have both involved is highly preferable. Even if one person is the primary one to put the children to bed, the other ought to take their turn on occasion.

If you and your spouse are not exactly on the same wavelength, do the best you can. Your spouse may not be averse to saying prayers, only to having to deal with bedtime. They may be exhausted and need some down time; they may want to relax for a few moments without either you or the children around. If your putting the children to bed gives your spouse a little bit of peace and quiet, that is fine. You deal with the bedtime routine; occasionally have your spouse come up for the prayers. That way they can participate in the process on occasion.

Sometimes people have bad experiences in the church growing up. Teaching your child about religious things may make your spouse nervous. They may worry about the various excesses that have sometimes accompanied religious zeal. But remind your spouse that these are exceptions rather than the rule. The answer is not to teach your child *nothing* about faith and God. The answer is to teach your child the *right things* about God. One important thing you can teach them is how to pray, so they have a foundation in God for their lives.

On one occasion, Jesus told the disciples to be "wise as serpents but harmless as doves" (*Matthew* 10:16). Jesus was telling the
136

disciples to use their wits, be full of goodwill, but cunning for what is good. This instruction applies to you as a parent. Be wise; use your wits and your good heart. Look for ways to engage your child in prayer, nurture their spiritual life, and teach them about God. Teaching your child to pray is one of the very best things you can give them. All the toys, presents, and other things you give your child will eventually break or be outgrown. When you teach your child to pray, however, you give them a gift for a lifetime. You give them a gift that will continue to provide them access to God, a release for their frustrations, and a source of guidance for their lives. The ability to pray is a gift second to none and has eternal consequences. Be wise and full of grace, but do not let anything stand in the way of teaching your child to pray!

One thing that will happen in these times of prayer is that you will have the opportunity for spiritual conversations with your child. The quiet time of conversation and prayer between you and your child will elicit comments, thoughts, and questions from them. While this gives you opportunities to guide your child's understanding, both about prayer and God, it may also raise anxieties for you. What if my child asks me a question I can't answer? What do I do then? This is an important subject that we will explore in detail in the next chapter.

9

QUESTIONS CHILDREN ASK

THE CURIOSITY OF CHILDREN

CHILDREN ARE CURIOUS, as well they should be. Everything is new for children and they explore the world with ceaseless interest. This is how children are wired and it helps them acquire a tremendous amount of knowledge in a relatively short span of time. By age four, children are linguistic geniuses in the way they can understand and construct sentences, yet they acquire this ability only by listening. Remarkable!

You should expect your child to be curious about things related to God. This is why, as you pray with your child, you will get questions from time to time. Some of them will be challenging. This possibility sometimes makes parents nervous because it has the potential to reveal the parent's lack of knowledge. As we said before, one reason we may shy away from talking to our children

139

about spiritual matters is the fear of spiritual "exposure." We may be afraid our lack of spiritual knowledge will be displayed in front of our children; therefore we hesitate to get into a situation where this might happen, such as one-on-one conversations with our child about spiritual things. These intimate conversations might give them a chance to ask a spiritually challenging question. Then what will we do?

Your parental anxieties, however, are not a good reason to avoid teaching your child to pray! Your anxieties *must not* keep you from engaging in this practice with your child; your anxieties are about *you* and not them. They make you much more nervous than they do your child, so do not let your apprehensions keep you from giving your children what they need in order to know God and love God. Your job as a parent is to do your part. God will help you along the way.

There are two things that will help you as a parent. One is that you may need to get up to speed in your biblical and theological understanding. If your religious comprehension is still at a kindergarten level, you need to change that situation. Just as you learned other subjects and mastered them, whether math, or history, or your occupation, you can learn about spiritual things. If you have learned the tools you need in other areas, such as your profession, you can increase your understanding in this area too. It is time to step up to the plate! Learn about Christianity and begin to be a student of the Bible, if you are not one already.

QUESTIONS ARE NOT BAD

What we want to explore, in this chapter and the next, is some sample questions and answers. My hope is that these will ease your fears and give you possible answers to difficult questions. We cannot touch on every question your child might ask, children can be quite creative, but we will try to give you an answer for some typical questions. I hope it will help to have some positive examples of how difficult questions can be answered.

There is a general principle to remember, especially for children who are young. It is, keep the answers short and simple. Give your child a simple answer they can connect with and leave it at that. Remember that children cannot process long complicated arguments. They think in concrete ways, so give them a short, concrete but honest answer; they will generally be satisfied with this. If they are not satisfied, they will say so or they will bring the question up again and you can take another shot at it. If you do not know the answer to something, tell them you need to think about it. Give them an answer the next night after you have had a chance to think your answer through.

Remember that questions are not bad. Questions are a part of true faith. Questions keep us honest; they keep us from believing things that are not true; they help us investigate things and discover the truth. Questions are always part of the life of faith. Martin Luther, the Protestant Reformer, said that only fanatics have no doubts. Real faith always asks questions and seeks answers. Real and honest faith always seeks greater understanding, and this is usually acquired through asking questions then searching for answers.

No matter how much you try to anticipate their questions, your child will inevitably ask something that will challenge you, whether it is, "Who did Cain marry," "What happened to the dinosaurs," or "Am I going to hell?" These are signs that they are thinking about their faith, and this is what you want. You want them to be thinking about what they believe. For that reason, questions are natural and a good thing. True faith does not want to be blind faith but have a solid, rational understanding of what it believes, so it knows it is founded on the truth.

Remember that the goal is faith; this is an important point to make. The goal is not an on-going set of questions without answers. The goal is authentic, confident, deeply held faith. That is why you need to give answers to your child's questions. As they get older their questions will become more subtle and sophisticated. This is why you need to continue to grow in your understanding of the faith and in the depth of your own spiritual life. You need to be on your own journey of faith, so you can guide your children along the way in theirs.

This means that if you have not started yet, this is a great time to re-energize your own life of faith. Make a commitment that you will seek to grow in prayer and understanding along with your child. Decide to learn more about Christianity, so you can explain it to your children. This will help you be better able to deal with questions of faith. As your child gets older he or she will continue to have questions that need your wisdom and guidance. To be a source of spiritual guidance to your child is a great privilege and opportunity. That is why we need to grow in faith along with them in order to be ready for more complicated questions as they grow up.

A REASONABLE FAITH

The Christian faith is reasonable; this needs to be understood. You do not have to shut down your mental faculties in order to be a Christian. This comes as a surprise to some people. Some have grown up believing that Christianity is anti-intellectual or that it defies reason. Does Christianity really make sense? Can it be rationally defended? The answer is that it does make sense and can be rationally defended. This does not mean that we understand everything there is to know about God. There are certainly limits to our knowledge about God, just as there are limits to our knowledge in many areas. Christianity recognizes that there are lots of things God has not told us, but there are plenty of things God *has* told us and these we can say with assurance.

How important is it to give our children answers? You might wonder if it is important for your children to discover things for themselves, especially where religion is concerned. Should you give them answers to their questions or let them struggle on their own? While it is important for children to grow up and be able to think for themselves, it is a terrible mistake to refuse children solid answers to their questions about faith. Sometimes parents think that it is best not to teach their children anything about God. That way they can grow up and make their own decisions about what they believe. This might seem wise, but it almost always guarantees that the child will grow up with *no faith*. This is *not* the approach you want to take with your child. As your child learns to pray, they will begin to grow in faith. You want this process to continue without them getting stuck or sidetracked. By giving them reasonable answers to their questions, you allow their faith to continue to grow in a natural way.

Think about how we learn other subjects. We do not learn math by not being given any answers. The same is true with history, geography, science, and almost every other subject. We learn the history of the discipline we are studying. We learn the fundamental facts of the subject. We master certain concepts that are necessary in order to understand the area. Does this mean that no one who has learned a subject will ever raise any questions about that subject? Of course not! But you must master the basic facts to be qualified to ask important questions. Albert Einstein could not have asked the questions he did and come up with new answers in the realm of physics, unless he had mastered the subject he wanted to advance. Scholars ask all sorts of questions in their fields, but they are qualified to do so only after years of intense study and mastery of their discipline.

Giving your child answers to their questions of faith does not mean that they will receive everything blindly once they become adults. On the contrary, a solid foundation for their faith will give them a platform from which to think about life, faith, and God. It will give them a place to stand as they think for themselves. It will give them the resources they need to be able to reason for themselves once they become an adult. Do not be afraid, however, to give your child a Christian worldview. Teach him or her the great truths of Christianity, that there is a God, who loves them, who created the world, who sent his Son into the world, whom we now know through the Holy Spirit, which God gives to those with faith, which gospel we are called to proclaim to the world. Teach these great truths, beliefs, and principles from the Bible and you will give your child a solid foundation from which to build a meaningful, productive, and happy life.

HOW DO WE KNOW GOD?

Let's review some basic facts about Christian belief. Christianity claims to have answers to many questions about life, faith, and God, but from where do these answers come? They come from the Bible. This is why the Bible is so important in Christianity; it is where God has told us what he wants us to know. Think about it this way. A person cannot really know you unless you reveal yourself to that person. They might know something about you, such as where you live and what kind of work you do, but they cannot really know you unless you open up to them. Unless you talk to them about your likes, dislikes, joys, and sorrows, they will not truly know you. This is what friendship is about. We open up our lives to someone and "let them in." We tell them who we are.

The question is, "How do we know about God?" One answer might be to simply *think* about God. As humans, we can certainly think about who God might be and what God might be like. History is littered with unsuccessful attempts to do so, however, because our reasoning is inadequate to understand a God who is invisible, almighty, omnipotent, and omniscient. Who is knowledgeable enough to figure God out?

So how do we know about God? The answer of the Bible is that we only know about God because God has *revealed himself.* God has chosen to make himself known. God is not silent but has spoken to the humans he created. Think about it from the point of view of a parent. Would you bring a child into the world then refuse to speak to your child? Of course not! So, would God create humans then refuse to say anything to them? This is a very important question. Some people suggest that God created the world, then left us on our own. God might be up there somewhere, but he is silent. Is this true? Christianity does not believe so. It believes that, like a good parent, God not only brought us into existence but has spoken to us in order to make his love and presence known.

How has God spoken to us? There are two ways. The first we call "General Revelation." This is a theological way of saying that God has given us a general knowledge of his presence, through various means. One means is through the created order. The Bible says that creation reveals the glory of God. It tells us something about the greatness and majesty of God. How magnificent must a

God be who can create a universe so large and beautiful as ours. Psalm 19 says that the heavens declare the glory of God; the skies proclaim the work of his hands. This is not to say that we can know everything about God simply from looking at the wonders of creation. There are still many questions left unanswered, yet we can recognize the presence of a powerful God who created a universe such as ours. Such a God must be majestic, creative, and worthy of our humble adoration.

Another way Christianity believes we recognize the presence of God is within our spirits. Since we have been created by God, there is something in the human spirit that recognizes its Creator and knows that there is a God. We hear the whisper of a voice from deep within our soul. It seems to be the echo of something deep and profound that calls to us and has an eternal resonance to it. It seems to say that we are made for something more, even if we are unsure of what that "more" is. The fifth century theologian, Augustine, said that there is a God-shaped void in the heart of every person. It yearns for God. In our moments of clarity we know in our hearts that there must be a God. Christianity says that both of these sources tell us something important about the reality of God. There is a God who ought to be acknowledged and worshipped.

SPECIAL REVELATION

As helpful as this general revelation of God is, there are still questions that remain. Who exactly is this powerful Creator? Why did he make the world and us? What does he require of us? Christianity believes that God has given us the answers to these questions in a more specific revelation of himself in the Bible. Theologians call this "Special Revelation." It gives clarity to the general revelation of God in the created order and comes to us through the Bible. The Bible is the written record of God's making himself known in human history in a more specific way than just the created order. Through specific persons and events, culminating in the coming of Jesus Christ, God has revealed himself with remarkable clarity. God has chosen to speak to us, not just in a general way, but in a more specific fashion, revealing himself in greater detail and with sufficient clarity that we can truly know who he is. In this more specific revelation, God has chosen to tell us about himself, about life, and about what he expects from us.

One of the things that is unique to Christianity is that God's revelation of himself to humanity has not been primarily through visions and ideas. One particular person did not hear God's voice and write down that revelation. While there are instances of this in the Bible, this is not primarily what the Bible contains. The problem with visions and revelations is that they are subjective and subject to human interpretation or misinterpretation. Should we really trust someone's personal vision as being reliable and authoritative on such an important subject as the nature and will of God, especially when it comes, primarily, through one person?

Christianity is different from many other religions in that it is a *historical* religion. That is, it believes God has revealed himself, not primarily through visions but in human history through people and
148

events. Christianity is a historical faith. This is a very important point. Christianity does not come to us just through ideas. Or through a mystical revelation from God to a single person. It comes in history. This is one reason we believe that our lives in the world and in human history are important. God declares that history is important because he has revealed himself to the world from within the realm of history.

The Bible is, among other things, the record of God's revealing himself, in events in human history. God speaks to the world he created in order to make his will known. This began with the story of creation and the calling of the people of Israel in the Old Testament. In this story, God revealed himself to people like Abraham, Jacob, Moses, David, Solomon, Isaiah, Jeremiah, and Daniel. God acted in the life of the nation of Israel, delivering them from their bondage in Egypt, giving them his laws on Mount Sinai, bringing them into the Promised Land, sending them the prophets, bringing them back from exile, and revealing himself through many other historical events. And though God has, at times, revealed himself to prophets through dreams and visions, these were always tied to historical events and moments in history.

Christianity believes that the culmination of God's revelation of himself in history is the coming of Jesus Christ and the beginnings of the church in the New Testament. God's revelation of himself comes to its climax in the person of Jesus Christ in whom we come to know God, not just in the life of a great teacher or mystic, but by seeing God himself come among us in flesh and blood.

149

That God revealed himself in history was certainly important to people in those moments, but it is also important to us now. God ordained that those moments were not just for one generation but revelatory for future generations. For that reason, he made sure that holy people wrote down the accounts of those events. It is these accounts that we have in the Bible. The Bible gives God's revelation of himself *permanence* and *extension*. It allows us and future generations to know God. It also extends God's revelation of himself around the world to people in every corner of the globe.

Christianity believes that the Bible is not just a record of God's revelation in history but an *inspired* record of those events. God inspired special people, most often prophets, to record in the Bible what we need to know to love and serve God. God has caused his words to be written in the Bible in such a way that, even many centuries later, God still speaks powerfully and relevantly through them.

THE VALUE OF THE BIBLE

The Bible gives us answers to the very fundamental questions we ask about life and ourselves. Because this is true, we have answers to give to our children. The answers the Bible gives us are trustworthy; that is what Christianity believes. While there is debate and discussion on many aspects of the Bible, the majority of what it teaches is straightforward and clear. The essential features of what we need to know about life and God are clear in the Bible.

It is from these clear teachings in the Bible that we have plenty of good answers to give to the questions our children raise. The Bible is a wealth of information to give us a clear picture of who God is and what he expects of us. When we come to things about which the Bible does not tell us a great deal, we simply say so. God has not revealed everything to us. We do not know the details of heaven, for example. When we come to these matters, we affirm what we do know and admit what has not been told us.

You may realize at this point that it might be important for you to be more familiar with the Bible than you are. How are you going to use the Bible's resources to answer your child's questions, when you don't know what is in the Bible? How can you answer their questions *about* the Bible when you don't really know what is *in* the Bible? A good way to do this is to get involved in your church. Look for ways to study the faith. Go to class or a small group. Begin to read the Bible yourself. Be intentional about finding ways to nurture your own faith and understanding. Visit us at www.creativechristianparenting.com for resources to help you grow in your faith.

As a way to help you think about how to answer difficult questions your child might ask, I have provided some questions and answers for you to consider. With each answer, I have given you some background information to help you think about why I gave the answer I did. We conclude this chapter with questions about God. In the next chapter, we continue with more questions and answers.

Questions About God

Here is a set of typical questions children might ask about God. I have provided an answer that you might use for each question. The rationale explains why the question is answered in the way it is. Remember to keep things simple when you answer questions your children ask, especially when they are young. As they get older you can go into more detail.

Question – "Who Is God?"

Answer – "God is the One who made all things, including the heavens and the earth. God also made you and me."

Rationale - One of the first things we can say about God is that God is the Creator. God made all things, including us. Theologians have made the point that God made all things "out of nothing." We create with existing materials. God created the universe without using anything that already existed. When explaining who God is to your child, a useful way to do so is to focus on God as the one who created all things.

Question – "Where does God live?"

Answer – "God lives in heaven and always watches over us."

Rationale - The Bible comes from a time in which a three-tiered universe did not seem odd. Heaven was above. The earth was where we live. Hell was below the earth. We do not think of the universe in this way today, but one should not overcomplicate things with children. To say that God lives in heaven is to say that God does not live on the earth and that God is a Spirit. God is not bound to flesh and blood like we are or to any other material existence. God is free. One important implication of God living in heaven is that, from there, he is able to see all things, including us. God sees us in order to watch over us and care for us. It is good for you child to know that God is watching over them to take care of them. Remind them of this from time to time.

QUESTION – "WHAT DOES GOD LOOK LIKE?"

Answer – "God is a Spirit and does not have a human body. No one knows what God looks like. What we know is that God is loving and good."

Rationale - God does not have a bodily existence, though he came at one point in the person of Jesus. God is a Spirit. This means that God is invisible and can be everywhere at the same time. We do not describe God by his appearance, as we do people. Instead, we describe God by his "attributes." In describing God, we say that God is omnipotent (all powerful), omnipresent (everywhere), omniscient (all knowing), perfectly loving, holy, pure, just, and the source of all beauty. It is important that children understand that God's very nature is not only power but love and goodness.

QUESTION – "WHO MADE GOD?"

Answer - "No one made God. God has always been here from before there was anything at all."

153

Rationale - This is one of the hardest things for anyone to get a handle on, adults included. We do not have much frame of reference for eternity. It is hard to imagine anyone, including God existing forever. But that is part of the mystery of God. One day, in the Kingdom of Heaven we may know the answer to this question, but for now we cannot explain how God exists from all eternity. But this is who God is, by definition. God is the one who has always been there and always will be. One of the things we learn, through Einstein's theories, is that time and space are interrelated. Without a material universe, time does not exist. For this reason, since God is not material, we can understand how God exists outside of time, since he exists outside the material universe. Before there was space and time, God was there. The book of *Genesis* says that, in the beginning, there was God (*Genesis* 1:1). To the question of God's eternal existence, the best we can say is that God has always been there and no one made God.

QUESTION – "DOES GOD LOVE EVERYONE?"

Answer – "Yes, God loves everyone, but God is displeased when people do bad things."

Rationale - The very nature of God is love. Love is not just the current mood of God or an aspect of his nature that may change in the future. God's very essence is love. This does not mean, however, that God approves of every human behavior. Because God is also holy, God tells us that we should always try to do the right thing. Children are very attuned to the existence of right and wrong.

Behind this question may be the question of whether God loves us when we do things that are wrong. It is important to affirm God's constant love for us but to help our children understand that God distinguishes between what is right and what is not.

10

MORE QUESTIONS AND ANSWERS

JESUS, CHURCH, HEAVEN, AND HELL

IN THE PREVIOUS CHAPTER, we began to look at sample questions children might ask and how to answer them. We said that questions are not bad; in fact they are a sign of a growing faith. Christian author Frederick Buechner said, "Doubts are the ants in the pants of faith." Doubts, like ants, irritate us out of our lethargy. They motivate us to get moving and seek answers to our questions. The good news about Christianity is that there are answers. In fact, Christianity has a long history, 2000 years old at this point, of thinking about God, faith, salvation, and every imaginable thing related to Christian belief. Whatever questions you have, people have already thought about them, suggested answers, had discussions, and come to conclusions. With a little study and research, you will discover a wealth of information about the reasonableness of Christianity. You will also discover that the Bible is more understandable and accessible than you may have imagined.

There was a wonderful idea that came out of the Protestant Reformation in the early 1500's. It was the idea that the Bible was "perspicuous." Perspicuous is a fancy word that means, "understandable, clear, transparent." Up until the time of the Reformation, people generally believed that only scholars could understand the Bible. Part of that was because the Bible only existed, in most places, in Latin, which only scholars could read. But it was also believed that the Bible was too complex for ordinary people to comprehend. "Leave the Bible to us," they said, "and we will tell you what you need to know." The Protestant Reformers came to believe that this was an unsatisfactory approach, because God had designed the Bible so that every person could read it and understand it. After all, during Jesus' ministry, the crowds listened to Jesus and understood him. For that reason, every person ought to have a Bible in their own language and be encouraged to read it. These developments led to what would become a characteristic Christian practice, personal Bible reading. Christianity encourages people to read the Bible at home, in their personal and private lives. That is, attending church should not be your only exposure to the Bible. You should have a Bible and read it on your own.

If reading the Bible on your own is new to you, let me give you some helpful suggestions. First, get a newer translation of the Bible. It is good if you still have your grandmother's Bible, but this is probably not the one you want to read. Get a new Bible that has print that is easy to read. Go to a bookstore or look online and find a

158

Bible you think you will enjoy reading. You don't need to spend a lot of money to find one. In this book, scripture passages have been from the English Standard Version translation of the Bible; this is a good one with which to start. Other good versions are the New International Version, the New Revised Standard Version, and the New King James Version.

Second, don't start at the beginning; start in the New Testament. The New Testament is more accessible and a better place to start than the Old Testament. Start with one of the Gospels; I would pick *Matthew, Mark*, or *Luke*. Read through the gospel a chapter, or half a chapter, each evening before you go to bed, or some other time during the day. There is no rush; read at a comfortable pace and take your time. You will be surprised how much of the Bible you will be able to read if you read a little bit each day. Once you have read one of the gospels, which contain the account of the life of Jesus, read the book of *Acts*, which tells the story of the first thirty years of the early church. Then read other books in the New Testament. After you have read a number of New Testament books, read the book of *Genesis* in the Old Testament and the first twenty chapters in the book of *Exodus*, which is the narrative portion of the book of *Exodus*. If you will do this, you will be on your way to starting to understand the Bible. At some point, read through the entire Bible. Make it your ultimate goal to read through the entire Bible three times. If you will read it through three times, you will get a feel for its flow, know its characters, and begin to truly understand it.

One thing you will discover about the Bible is that it is different types of literature. Only about half of it is narrative, that is, historical accounts. Narrative is easier to read because there is a plot and story line. In narratives, there are people involved and events taking place. The gospel accounts of the life of Jesus are historical narratives, for example; they tell the story of the life of Jesus and what he did. Other parts of the Bible are not narrative, however. The Bible also contains laws, proverbs, prayers, poetry, prophecies, and something called apocalyptic literature. This makes the Bible interesting but also means that you have to get used to reading different types of literature in the Bible. Don't panic. You will get used to these different types of literature, especially if you start in the narrative sections, as I have suggested, and ease into the rest of the Bible from there.

If at all possible, strive to become a student of the Bible. If you do, it will help you answer your child's questions. To be able to effectively pass Christian knowledge on to your child ought to be incentive for you to put some effort into learning the Bible yourself and coming to understand the Christian faith. You will be surprised, however, how quickly you can increase your knowledge if you will put out a little effort. Visit us at www.creativechristianparenting.com for resources to help you understand the Bible, learn Christian belief, and improve your parenting skills.

As we said, previously, there are people who don't teach their children about God. Some people think it's not their job. Others don't realize they need to. Some think the church will do it. Others are afraid of their children getting caught up in religious excesses. Christian parents however, are supposed to teach their children about God and teach them the right things about God. Your job is to help your child develop a true, balanced, healthy understanding of God, themselves, and the world. As you are talking with your child in the evening, just before you say your prayers together, you have a natural opportunity to field their questions and teach them about the person, nature, and will of God. As you answer their questions about their faith, you have a marvelous opportunity to help them understand the greatness of God and the depth of his love for them and others.

Here are some additional sample questions and answers.

QUESTIONS ABOUT JESUS

QUESTION – "WHO IS JESUS?"

Answer – "Jesus is God's Son. God sent Jesus to become human and to give his life for our sins."

Rationale - Children understand the relationship between a child and a parent. The child is like the parent but not exactly. You do not have to get into the Trinity with a child until they become teenagers. It is usually enough for them to know that Jesus is the Son of God. We say that we are also children of God, through Jesus, but we are "adopted" children of God. Jesus is God's only "natural" Son. To describe Jesus as the Son of God makes sense to children.

QUESTION – "WHO IS GOD, JESUS OR GOD?"

Answer - "Both are God. God is our Father in heaven. Jesus is God's Son."

Rationale - The doctrine of the Trinity can get confusing and it took the church three centuries to come up with language to express it. The way we express it is to say that we worship one God in three persons. This means God has relationship within himself. God has love within himself that isn't merely self-love. The Father, the Son, and the Spirit are all fully God but are not three Gods. They are one God and exist in each other; you never find one present without the others. There are functions that are primarily attributed to each: Creation to the Father, Redemption to the Son, Sustaining Power to the Spirit. Though our language is approximate, we say that both Jesus and the Father are God and Jesus is God's Son.

QUESTION – "WHEN DID GOD CREATE JESUS?"

Answer - "God did not create Jesus, like he created the universe and us. Jesus has always been there. Since Jesus is God, Jesus has been with the Father from before time."

Rationale - The language the Bible uses is that Jesus in God's only "begotten" Son. This is a word that signifies a coming forth rather than creation or birth. Jesus was not begotten in history or time, as we understand it, however. Jesus is the only begotten Son of God from *before* time. All this is to say that Jesus is not part of creation as is the rest of the universe. He is not a created being, like the angels. In addition, there is no time when Jesus did not exist. The best answer is to say that Jesus is not created, like we have been created. Jesus is different and has been God and been with God from the beginning.

QUESTION – "DID JESUS REALLY DO MIRACLES?"

Answer - "Yes, since Jesus was God's Son, he could heal people, calm the stormy seas, and do all kinds of miracles."

Rationale - Jesus' ministry was not primarily about doing miracles yet they were a part of his ministry. His miracles helped draw the crowds to hear his teachings; they also confirmed his claim to be the Son of God. Jesus did miracles in such quantity and of such difficulty that no other person has ever been able to do the same things. This is what you would expect, however, if God came to earth in human form. You would expect God to be able to display power over the natural world and over human diseases. If we believe that God came in human form in the person of Jesus, we can believe that Jesus did the miracles that are recorded in the Bible.

QUESTION – "HOW LONG DID JESUS LIVE?"

Answer – "Jesus lived about 33 years. He started his public ministry when he was about 30 years old. It lasted for 3 years. Jesus accomplished more in just 3 years than anyone else has ever accomplished in a lifetime."

Rationale - We do not have exact dates for either the birth or death of Jesus. Calendars were not kept as accurately then as they are now. We think that the birth of Jesus was 4-5 B.C. and his death around

29 A.D. When the Gregorian calendar was developed, they tried to set the birth of Jesus at 0 A.D., but missed it by a few years. We know that Jesus' ministry was about 3 years long because of the number of times he went to the yearly Passover festival in Jerusalem, as recorded in the Gospel of John.

QUESTION – "DID IT HURT WHEN JESUS DIED ON THE CROSS?"

Answer – "Yes. It hurt him just as much as it would hurt us. In addition Jesus was carrying the weight of our sins in his soul. This was an additional terrible burden."

Rationale - If Jesus was fully human, then his ordeal on the cross was as painful as it would be for anyone. The Father did not shield him from the pain; he experienced it fully; any other belief makes Jesus only "appear" human. Christian theology has always believed that Jesus was both fully human and fully God. This means that Jesus felt real and excruciating pain on the cross.

QUESTION – "DID JESUS REALLY RISE FROM THE DEAD?"

Answer – "Yes, after being crucified and dying, Jesus was buried. On the third day afterwards, God raised Jesus back to life to demonstrate that he was really the Son of God."

Rationale - There is a great deal of evidence that Jesus rose from the dead. This is not the kind of event that is repeatable. That is, you cannot repeat the resurrection in a laboratory. The resurrection is a historical event that one can examine, as a jury examines evidence in a courtroom, to determine what actually happened. Examining the resurrection this way makes it extremely credible as a historical event. Some of the historical evidence for the bodily resurrection of Jesus is listed below:

- If the story of the resurrection were made up, the women would not have been the first ones to whom Jesus appeared. It makes the disciples look bad.

- The disciples were slow to believe, as anyone would be who was told that someone had risen from the dead. In normal experience, people do not rise from the dead, so it would take very convincing evidence. The disciples were hard to convince, yet the disciples did come to believe. It makes sense that their belief came only as a result of their seeing the risen Christ themselves. The gospels say this is exactly what happened.

- Everyone acknowledged that the tomb was empty, yet dead bodies are notoriously difficult to hide. If the body had just been moved or stolen, the religious authorities would have found it. Parading the body of Jesus through the streets of Jerusalem would have stopped the entire "Jesus movement," if the religious authorities could have found it. The body was never discovered, however, because there wasn't one. Jesus had risen.

- The story that the disciples stole the body while the soldiers slept is not credible. Soldiers did not sleep on duty, at least not all of them. Their life depended on their keeping their prisoner safe. They were highly trained to stay awake and would have done so in shifts. It is also not credible to think that the stone could have been rolled back quietly enough to keep them from waking. In addition, if they were asleep, how would the soldiers know who stole the body?

- The gospel of John reports that the linen cloths that were wrapped around Jesus were still in the tomb, with the head piece lying by itself. If someone had stolen the body, they would not have taken the time to unwrap the grave cloths. It would have been quicker to take the body wrapped up. It would also have been cleaner since Jesus would certainly have been bloody from the scourging and crucifixion. The one thing that makes sense is that Jesus or an angel unwrapped the grave cloths after he rose or that he simply vanished out of them when he rose, leaving them where he lay.

- The change in the disciples was remarkable. On Saturday after the crucifixion, they were confused and dejected. Fifty days later, they would be bold, confident, and willing to risk their lives to proclaim Christ's resurrection. What precipitated the change? They must have had something dramatic happen that completely changed them. The one reasonable possibility is that they saw the risen Christ. They saw him and knew that he had risen from the dead. When the Holy Spirit descended on the church, it gave them the power to give confident witness to what they knew to be true.

- The existence of the Christian Church today is evidence that Christ still lives. The church would never have come into existence without the resurrection. The resurrection was the centerpiece of the message of the early church. The church exists and thrives today because the living Christ continues to call it into existence and empower it.

QUESTIONS ABOUT HEAVEN AND HELL

QUESTION – "AM I GOING TO HEAVEN?"

Answer – "Yes. Everyone who believes in Jesus is going to heaven."

Rationale - When children hear about heaven and hell it makes an impression. Even a casual acquaintance with the subject raises basic questions. Children want to be sure they are going to heaven and not to hell. The best thing to do is assure them that they are going to heaven, because of their faith in Jesus. Of course a child has a limited faith. He or she believes in a childlike and naïve way. But nevertheless this is belief. You want to nurture this blossoming faith by affirming what faith they have and continuing to cultivate it. If you have been doing some basic things, like reading them stories from a children's Bible, they probably have a basic knowledge about Jesus. They have probably not even imagined anything other than believing in him. *Of course* they believe in him because that is what one is supposed to do. Especially in their younger years, assure them that God loves them and that they are going to heaven because

167

of their faith in Jesus. Trust God to help that faith develop as they grow up.

QUESTION – "AM I GOING TO HELL? I SOMETIMES DO BAD THINGS."

Answer – "Everyone does things that are wrong, but that is why Jesus came. He came to die for our sins and to forgive us. We go to heaven because we believe in Jesus. God is not going to send you to hell."

Rationale - When children begin to feel their conscience, they become aware of things they do that are wrong. This is a good thing. One of the goals of good parenting is to help your child develop, in their conscience, a sense of right and wrong. But this also raises the question of going to hell. You do not want to casually dismiss their sensitive consciences, but it is a good time to remind them again that Jesus' death on the cross provides us forgiveness. It is also a good time to tell them that they can tell God they are sorry for something they have done. They can ask Jesus to forgive them and he will. Again it is important to assure them they are going to heaven and not to hell. This assurance is biblical. Theologically it is called the Doctrine of Assurance. It says that we can be assured of our salvation, because of our faith in Christ. Because we are assured of our salvation, we serve God out of love and gratitude, not out of fear. This is good to begin to implant in your child's heart. As we grow in faith, the Holy Spirit confirms this feeling in our hearts, inwardly assuring us that we are indeed children of God. You also want to help your child picture God as a loving Father, not as an angry Judge.

QUESTION – "IS MY FRIEND WHO DOES NOT BELIEVE IN JESUS GOING TO HELL?"

Answer – "It is not for us to say who is going to hell. That is God's job. It is our job to tell other people about Jesus. Maybe we can invite your friend to our church. God wants everyone to know about him."

Rationale - God is the one who decides who goes to hell. It is not our job, thank goodness. The Bible also says that God wants everyone to be saved. The best approach to this question is to do something proactive to invite the friend to church, if possible. Think about some activity in church to which you can invite them, such as a children's outing, or Vacation Bible School, or other activity. It might be a way to draw them and their family into a relationship with Christ. It is a good thing to help your child begin to think about reaching out to others who do not know Christ.

QUESTION – "WHAT IS HEAVEN LIKE?"

Answer – "We do not know exactly what heaven is like except that we are with God and with all the angels and there is no sadness or pain. It is a place where we are happy all the time."

Rationale - The Bible gives us some glimpses into heaven but never a complete description of it. The Bible does say, however, that its joy is greater than our eyes have seen, our ears have heard about, or our hearts have imagined. Heaven is not a place where we sit on a cloud and play a harp all day. There will be something engaging to do in heaven. In addition to worshipping God, we will be in relationship with the saints and angels. Most theologians think we will have something to do that uses our gifts and talents. It will be a perfect realm where there is no more sin, sickness, sorrow, or death. Best of all we will be in perfect relationship with God and that will fill our lives with joy, peace, and meaning.

QUESTION – "WHAT IS HELL LIKE?"

Answer – "Hell is the place people go who do not want to be with God and any place without God will be full of sadness, loneliness, and pain."

Rationale - As with heaven, the Bible does not give us a full description of hell, but it repeatedly uses the image of fire. It is like burning in fire all the time. In other words, it is the worst thing one can imagine. The essence of hell is being without God. To be without God is to be lonely, sad, and in pain. Theologians through the centuries have speculated, with differing opinions, as to whether the torments of hell are physical, emotional, spiritual, or all three. Hell is not a place to be preoccupied with except as an incentive to believe in Jesus and serve him faithfully.

Question – "Will God really send people to hell?"

Answer – "The Bible seems to say that God will send people to hell but not because God is mean. God is full of love, but, in the end, everyone will get what they deserve. Some people who do terrible things will be sentenced to hell.

Rationale - Heaven and hell are, in one sense, about the issue of justice. The Bible says that God is the judge of humankind and everyone must stand before him. That there is both a heaven and hell says that God will ultimately mete out true justice. We recognize that, in this life, justice is not always done. The wicked prosper; the righteous have bad things happen. People do not always get true justice. So if there is to be any true and final justice, it must come after this life and it must come from God. This is what the idea of the final judgment is all about; in the end there will be justice for everyone. God will set everything right and judge everyone fairly. This is why the Bible says it is not in vain to serve God. It is also why the fear of God, which means the fear of disobeying God's laws, is the beginning of wisdom.

Question – "Does the Bible say that only 144,000 are going to heaven?"

Answer – "No, the Bible does not say that. The book of Revelation has one section in which 144,000 Jewish people are saved. But these are not the only people saved. This number may not be meant to be an exact number but symbolize completeness. It says that, in the end, a large number of Jewish people will be saved.

Rationale - The numbers in the book of Revelation are mysterious. Biblical interpreters differ as to whether the numbers are symbolic or literal, and there are sounds reasons for both opinions. The number 144,000 comes from a section in the book of *Revelation* (*Revelation* 7:4, 14:1, 3) in which people are saved from the various tribes of Israel. If it does not signify an exact number, it signals that a great many people will be saved, from each of the tribes of the nation. Whatever these numbers mean, these are not the only people saved. They are just one example of many people who will stand before God as having served him well.

QUESTION – "DO I HAVE TO BE GOOD TO GO TO HEAVEN?"

Answer – "What gets us into heaven is our faith in Jesus. We should be good because we love him and want to please him, and as a way of saying thank you for what he has done for us."

Rationale - The Christian life should be one of good moral character, but it is not our good moral character that gets us into heaven. No one is perfect and because of this we all fall under the condemnation of sin. That is why Jesus came; Jesus came so we might be forgiven. What he asks us to do is have faith in him. John 3:16, says that "whoever believes in him will not perish but have eternal life." This is a great promise and ought to elicit humility and gratitude in us. It is from this gratitude that we find the motivation to live a life of solid Christian character.

QUESTION – "IS MY PET GOING TO HEAVEN?"

Answer – "We do not know if pets go to heaven or not. We do know that God seems to have lots of creatures in heaven as well as angels. It is possible that pets go to heaven."

Rationale - Every child loves their pet. When a pet dies, it is a difficult moment. The truth is that we do not know if pets go to heaven. Traditionally, theology says, "No." Pets do not have souls as we do; they are not made in the image and likeness of God as we are; they do not stand before God to answer for their actions, either good or bad. For that reason, it has generally been understood that animals do not have souls, are not morally culpable, and do not have an eternal existence. We certainly hope, for example, that mosquitos will not exist in heaven. That being said, the Bible is full of visions of heaven in which there are all sorts of creatures. See *Isaiah* 6, for example. God created animals and made some of them so they could be domesticated and serve as pets. One can be on solid ground saying that the glimpses we have of heaven include creatures that are neither angels nor humans. Their role always seems to be to give glory to God. It would be going too far to say that these are God's pets; we do not know their role. Heaven will be an amazing and wondrous place. God has made animals for the good of the world and our selves. Heaven will be filled with many things that will fill us with joy. Whether that includes pets is something we do not know.

QUESTIONS ABOUT CHURCH

QUESTION – "WHY DO I HAVE TO GO TO CHURCH?"

Answer – "Because it is where we learn about God."

Rationale - God gave us the church. Jesus established the church. Though the church is a human institution, it does not originate as a human idea. It is God's idea for our welfare. Church is the vehicle God created for people to learn about himself, about faith, about Jesus, and about how we ought to live. If God thought the church a good idea, we should take advantage of this means of grace.

QUESTION – "IF GOD IS EVERYWHERE WHY IS IT IMPORTANT TO GO TO CHURCH?"

Answer – "Because church is where there are people to teach us and help us learn. We need teachers who will help us understand the Bible."

Rationale - God is everywhere. We can experience God anywhere, in the mountains, at the beach, and even on a golf course. But we are more likely to learn about God by being in Sunday School, attending worship, and meeting with other Christians than we are playing golf, sleeping in, or watching television. When we and our children attend church we are more likely to learn the lessons of the faith and how to apply them to our lives.

QUESTION – "WHY IS CHURCH SOMETIMES BORING?"

Answer – "Church may sometimes seem boring, but I expect you to pay attention and learn something."

Rationale - Even the most exciting church seems boring to children at times; children are easily bored. Think back to your own childhood. Anything that required you to sit still was considered boring. Your job as a parent, however, is not to entertain your child. Neither is it the job of the church to compete with the latest video game for excitement. The job of the church is to teach and impart the faith; the job of the child is to be an attentive learner. Do not fall into the trap of placing the entire burden on the church to be exciting. Expect your child to pay attention and learn. This is what we require of them at school. Why should church be any different?

QUESTION – "WHY DO THEY TAKE AN OFFERING AT CHURCH?"

Answer – "The offerings we give help support the work of the church. They are also a practical way we say thank you to God for his many material blessings."

Rationale - The Bible tells us to give back to God. One way we do this is through giving our financial resources. We might think it enough just to give our time and talents. These are very important but not the entire picture. Jesus said, "Where your treasure is, there will your heart be also." We can get obsessed with money and it can assume an inordinate place in our life. One way to lessen money's allure is to give some back to God. It helps put our heart in the right place and enables us to participate in the work of God through our local congregation. It is a good practice to give to your local church and even children should begin to learn this practice. The financial giving of the people of the church is the way God has ordained that the church will be supported and its work sustained. Be a faithful giver to your congregation and set a good example for your children to follow when they grow up.

QUESTION – "WHY ARE THERE SO MANY DIFFERENT DENOMINATIONS?"

Answer – "There are many denominations because people are different. Some people like one thing; others like another. People also understand parts of the Bible in different ways. We all love God and want to follow God; we just do it slightly differently."

Rationale - The variety of denominations has to do with both taste and difference of opinion. Some people think the multitude of denominations is a great scandal and a blight on the witness of Christianity. That might be true, but denominations are a reality. It is better not to disparage other denominations to your child. Most denominations have their strengths and weaknesses. Most do some things well and others less well. Be gracious about other churches and tell your child what you like about your church and denomination. Help them learn to love all Christians and appreciate the things your church or denomination does well.

QUESTION – "DO WE HAVE TO GO TO CHURCH EVERY SUNDAY?"

Answer – "Yes. If we are not sick or out of town, we are going to church on Sunday."

Rationale - You may not be quite as regular as this answer indicates. Give an answer appropriate to your situation. If you are not regular in church, however, consider the advantages of doing so. Your child picks up on what is important to you. They pick up on what you are really committed to. Why not make a commitment to be regular in church! Why be a lukewarm or half-hearted Christian? Remember that you are developing habits in your child. If they have good experiences in the church at an early age, they will remember those when they get older. If they find friends in church, learn about God in church, and get positive reinforcement in church, they will come to love the church. Help them have a good experience in church. This means that you need to be an active member of your congregation. Everyone needs the church; you do and they do. Since they will need to be involved in the church all their life, start them in the habit now. It is also a great mistake that will have far reaching consequences, to take your family out of church. No matter what problems you may have with the church, do not leave it. If you must find a new church, do so, and be committed to it.

MISCELLANEOUS QUESTIONS

QUESTION – "DID ADAM HAVE A BELLY BUTTON?"

Answer - "We don't know. We will have to ask Adam when we get to heaven."

Rationale - Your answer here will depend on exactly how you interpret the creation account in *Genesis* 1. If you want to take a literal approach, you might say that Adam did *not* have a belly button, because he was not born from a mother. God created Adam from the dust and he would not have had a belly button. You may simply want to say that we do not know. The important things about the story of Adam and Eve are: God's creation of us, as male and female, in his own image, to work in his world, and be in communion with him. These kinds of questions satisfy you child's intellectual curiosity but are not integral to helping them understand God. For this type of question, it is okay to say, "We don't know."

QUESTION – "DOES GOD EVER SLEEP?"

Answer – "No, God never sleeps. As humans, we need to sleep, but God does not. He watches over us night and day. He takes care of the world and always is there to hear us when we pray.

Rationale - As humans we need to rest, let go of the problems of the day, and allow sleep to renew our minds and spirits. God does not need this. This makes sense since the need for rest is a function of bodily existence. Our bodies get tired, but God is a Spirit and not subject to human limitations. One of the amazing characteristics of God is that he is always available to us to when we pray. Any time
178

of day or night, God is there. Not only does God watch over us, twenty-four hours a day but he constantly maintains his providential care for our world and universe.

QUESTION – "WHAT ABOUT DINOSAURS? WHERE DO THEY FIT INTO THE BIBLE?"

Answer – "We don't know when the dinosaurs existed. They probably died out before the Bible was written."

Rationale - Children are fascinated with dinosaurs and quite frankly, who isn't. What can we say about dinosaurs? There are a number of possible answers. One is simply to say that dinosaurs lived a long time ago, before the Bible was written. You can say that God loves making things and he must have had a lot of fun making the dinosaurs. They died out, however, before most of the Bible was written, even before Adam and Eve were born. This is an answer that agrees with modern scientific views. Another answer is to say that the dinosaurs probably died in the flood. Another is to say that they died shortly after getting out of the Ark because the climate changed after the flood. Could dinosaurs get into the Ark? Only if they were babies, but nothing says that baby dinosaurs could not have been taken on the Ark. Here is a place where it is okay to say, "We don't know," especially since that is a truthful answer.

QUESTION – "WHO DID CAIN MARRY?"

Answer - "We don't know who Cain married. Perhaps Adam and Eve had other children before Cain and Abel."

Rationale – The Bible says that Adam and Eve were the first people. When they were cast out of the Garden of Eden after eating the forbidden fruit, they had two children, Cain and Abel. After Cain killed his brother Abel, God punished him by sending him away. Chapter 4 of *Genesis* says that Cain eventually met his wife and they had children. Here is the difficult question, however. If Adam and Eve were the first people, where did Cain's wife come from? This is a place where the Bible has some mystery to it and we can't give an answer more definitive than the information the Bible gives us. There are several possibilities. The first is that Adam and Eve had children before they fell from grace in *Genesis* 3, and Cain married one of them. In the curse, in *Genesis* 3, God tells Eve that he will "increase" her pain in childbearing (*Genesis* 3:16). This sounds like she has already been through the process of bearing children. The second possibility is that Cain married one of the children Adam and Eve had after the fall, or a daughter that came from the marriages of some of those children. The book of *Genesis* says that Adam and Eve had a number of other children who are not named in the Bible. Cain's marriage might have been many years later after one of those children had grown to a marriageable age. If your child thinks about this much, they will realize that this has Cain potentially marrying one of his sisters, which they will probably find creepy. So maybe the best answer is simply to say that this is something we just don't understand and leave it at that. There is a lot of mystery to this ancient biblical time.

SUMMARY

I hope these two chapters will give you confidence in answering your child's difficult questions about God, Jesus, church, heaven, and hell. When asked a difficult question, you may be tempted to say, "We'll have to ask the pastor that question." I would encourage you not to take this approach, however. Give the answer a shot yourself! It is better for you to give your child an answer, if at all possible. You will be surprised how well you will do, if you will make the attempt. Give them your best answer. You can ask your pastor later if you need to but see what you can do first. Most likely, you will do much better than you think. Your child will love you and respect you for it and you will have the privilege of being one of the primary people who teaches your child about God.

11

NEXT STEPS IN PRAYER WITH YOUR CHILD

A LITTLE AT A TIME

W E HAVE STARTED WITH a simple plan. As our child grows up, however, we want them to grow in the practice of prayer. Once they begin to master the basic aspects of prayer, what should we do? If you start this process with your child at the age of four or five, you will have many years to pray with your child before they leave home for college or their career. Because of this, you have plenty of time to help your child grow in faith and in their relationship with God. Be patient and take it one step at a time.

The goal is for our children to grow in their experience of God. We are not so much after their becoming better at prayer, as if prayer was a technique to be learned. We want them to experience an increasing level of God's presence in their lives. The good news is that the simple practice of praying with your child, over a number of years, will make a tremendous impact. This is not because of something you will do but the presence and work of the Holy Spirit. God will make himself known to them and they will come into their own relationship with him.

When our children went to school and started to learn to read, my wife and I were reminded how difficult learning to read is. You take it for granted once you know how to do it, but I remember the children bringing home lists of words to memorize. They had to learn how to sound out the words. It took a long time to be able to recognize, on sight, words that would later be obvious to them. Before long, however, they began to read without even thinking about it. This reminds us that almost everything can be learned, even complex things, if you take them one small piece of information at a time.

How do you as a parent, help your child continue to learn about God as they start their life of prayer? The answer is that you do it one piece at a time. The prophet Isaiah said that his knowledge of God came, "precept upon precept, precept upon precept, line upon line, line upon line, here a little, there a little" (*Isaiah* 28:10). Just like we learn our lessons in school, we learn about our faith one piece at a time, both in terms of knowledge and experience. If you can teach your child about God in small manageable pieces, you will eventually be able to impart to them a great amount of information and lead them into a variety of rich spiritual experiences.

PRAYERS OF CONFESSION

We mentioned in a previous chapter that one important type of prayer is "Prayers of Confession." We need to say more about this kind of prayer as it relates to your child. Every person needs to make prayers of confession part of their life with God. This is because everyone sins; for that reason, we all need to ask forgiveness from God. It is prayers of confession that enable us to reflect on our failures, release our guilt to God, and receive his assurance of pardon.

Because we all need forgiveness, a standard practice down through the centuries has been to make confession part of our regular prayers, especially our evening prayers. Traditionally, in our morning prayers, we think about our day and ask God for grace to meet our challenges. In the evening we review our day, think about where we fell short, and ask forgiveness for our failings. We reflect on our failures, think about our thoughts, words, and actions, admit our shortcomings, and ask for forgiveness and grace. The Bible assures us that, when we confess with an honest and humble heart, God forgives our sins. This wipes clean the slate between God and us and gets us ready for a peaceful night's sleep, so we can begin fresh in the morning.

When it comes to confessing our sins, do we need to confess every sin in order to be forgiven? What if we can't remember them all? The good news is that we do *not* have to remember and confess every sin in order to be forgiven. Christianity believes that, in

Christ, we are forgiven all our sins. This is a good thing since we can never recall and confess all our sins. Most of us can't remember what we had for lunch two days ago; how are we going to remember all the sins we have ever committed? There are just too many and, in addition, we are often unaware of things we do that fall short of God's will. We sin when we don't even realize it. By the grace of God, however, we are completely forgiven through the grace of Jesus Christ. It is still a good idea to confess specific sins of which we are aware, however. To name our missteps, weaknesses, and failures before God helps *us* reflect on how we might do better. It also creates within us a humility that is necessary and appropriate.

How then do we teach our children to confess their sins to God? There are several ways. One is to look for an opportunity for them to confess something of which you are both aware. It might be a situation, for example, in which they have gotten into a disagreement (verbal or physical) with a sibling or friend. This is a good opportunity to say, "Why don't we ask God tonight to forgive us our sins today. You might want to tell God you're sorry for hitting your brother." This might prompt some conversation or response from your child, such as: "Yes, but he started it." This creates a teaching moment both to talk about the problem and to let your child vent if they need to. This can be an opportunity for your child to talk about things that are bothering them. Allow what conversation is needed, but eventually turn the conversation back to your child's responsibility. "Yes, but what did you do wrong in this situation?" After they answer (and they may need some prompting and guidance), you can say, "You tell God, then what *you* did wrong

186

and ask for help to do better." You may need to help them with the wording. You might say, "Say something like, 'God, I'm sorry I got so mad at my brother and I'm sorry I hit him.'" Even if they pray this prayer a bit grudgingly, it still serves a useful purpose for them to do so.

This kind of conversation and this small act of confession on your child's part is healthy. It helps them understand that they fall short of God's will in many ways. Therefore they need to turn to God for forgiveness and grace. Our need for forgiveness is one of those things that keeps us coming back to God. People who think they don't need forgiveness, begin to think they do not need God. That is a terrible misjudgment and one we do not want our children to make.

From an early age we tried to implant within our children's hearts the simple principle – always tell the truth. I have said this to them on many occasions, especially when I was not sure they were doing so, "Remember, always tell the truth." Our children won't always tell us everything; but we want them to learn to value the truth and be able to be totally honest with God.

We have some short phrases we use as prayers at the end of our prayers each evening. I will talk about these in the next chapter. One of the phrases we say each night at the end of our prayers is, "Forgive me my sins." We say it before we say, "Amen." We each say it as a kind of closing to our prayers each night along with, "Dear God I love you very much." We say, "Forgive me my sins. Dear God, I love you very much. Amen."

This is not a very specific prayer. In fact it can become somewhat rote, but it keeps before the child the idea that forgiveness is something we ought to pray about regularly. This is certainly the case, since the Lord's Prayer includes it. One of the phrases in the Lord's Prayer is, "Forgive us our sins as we forgive those who sin against us." Asking forgiveness for our sins is one of the central requests Jesus taught us to make. As a family, we have made this simple phrase, "Forgive me my sins," a regular part of our prayers. It has helped give our children an appropriate sense of humility in relation to God. "Forgive me my sins. Dear God, I love you very much. Amen."

DEVELOPING A PRAYER LIST

Most of us make lists. We make grocery lists, to-do lists, and task lists at work. We do these because there are important things we don't want to forget. There is a place for lists in your life of prayer. Maybe you have had someone say to you, "Please pray for me." Maybe you said, in reply, "I will." But then what happens? Well, you *don't* remember. When we promise to pray for someone, we are usually sincere; we *intend* to pray for them. But the next time we remember the request may be the next time we see the person who asked us to pray for them. *Then* we remember that we were supposed to pray for them. Ouch!

A prayer list is a good practice because it helps us remember people for whom we should pray or for whom we have promised to pray. This is a practice you can start with your child at some point. Here is a simple method for doing this with your child. Take an index card, either 3 x 5, or 4 x 6, or simply a piece of paper. Use this as your prayer list and place it near your child's bed, on the nightstand, in your child's Bible, or somewhere you will see it occasionally. Write on it the names of people for whom you want to pray. Then look at it several times during the week as a way to remember to pray for the people on your list. This is a simple and workable method you can use with your child.

If you want to be a little more sophisticated about it, you can write the days of the week on the card or piece of paper. Then pick one thing to remember to pray for each day. For example, on Sundays pray for your family and everyone's endeavors for the week ahead. On Mondays, pray for our nation, its safety, its spiritual health, and its leaders. On Tuesdays pray for extended family and relatives. On Wednesday pray for people you know who are sick and in need. On Thursday, again pray for the needs of your family. On Friday, give thanks to God for all God's blessings. On Saturday, pray for the church around the world, your church in particular, and your church's pastors and other leaders. At night you can remind your child of the subject of the day, saying something like, "Tonight we pray for our church and its pastors. Try to remember to pray for them in your prayers." You can use a weekly pattern like this or develop one of your own. This is a good way to give your child's prayers some variety and to remember to pray for things you and they ought to pray for on a regular basis.

Having a prayer list is a very simple way to develop a good habit in your child. When a prayer gets answered, in some way that is obvious, you can point it out. You might even put a star or asterisk by the name of the person as a reminder of the answer. When you fill up the card, don't throw it away. Put a date on it and put it in a drawer. As the years go by, you can pull the prayer cards out to look at them. They will remind you and your child of some of the people you have prayed for and some of the answers you have received.

Maybe one thing realize at this point is that there is no one way to pray or one set way to do so. Author Richard Foster has an intriguing idea. He says that we can create what he calls "prayer experiments." These are little prayer projects, each of which might last a day or a week but that expand our ability to pray and our experience of prayer. For example, you might decide that you will pray for the people in the car in front of you every time you stop at a traffic light. Why do this? Well, why not? Why not pray for the people in the car in front of you? It will give you a new way to pray and maybe even help some people who need your prayers. Does this mean you will do this forever? No, just for a day or maybe a week. One day you might decide you will pray for some stranger you see during the day, or on TV, or that you read about online. Say a quick prayer for them and ask God to bless them. Or you might decide that one entire day, you will especially thank God for one particular thing, such as sufficient food to eat, or for your job, or your friends, etc. You can teach your children to do this as well. Say, "Today at school, pray for someone you don't normally associate with." Or,

"Today, thank God for every one of your teachers and pray for them." Or "Today pray for some people that don't have many friends." This will expand their experience of prayer and also give them a tender heart toward others.

FAITH AND PRAYER

One of the things that is clear in the New Testament is that we are encouraged to have faith. There is a wonderful definition of faith in *Hebrews* 11, verse 6, and it is attached to the practice of prayer. It says, "And without faith, it is impossible to please him, for whoever would draw near to God must believe that he exists and that he rewards those who seek him." This says that faith is believing that God exists and that he will respond with grace toward those who seek him.

What exactly is faith? It is conviction. It is a firm assurance that the promises in the scriptures are true, not just for others, but for ourselves. Whereas hope is believing in things that have not yet happened, faith is believing in things we cannot see. Faith is what arises in us when we hear the promises of God to us in the Bible and believe them to be true. That faith lives in us is ultimately not a human work but something given to us by the Holy Spirit. Through the process of praying with your child and teaching them about God, you will have the wonderful opportunity to watch faith grow in them. There is no greater or more fulfilling thing you can experience as a parent!

What does faith mean in connection to prayer? It simply means that we believe God is present with us when we pray and listening to our prayers. This is something we are able to say with complete confidence; God is listening to us when we pray! This is clearly affirmed throughout scripture; God listens when we pray. Help your child know this and, from time to time, reassure your child about this.

How then do we act on this belief? One way is to be consistent in our prayers. Unless there is some very unusual circumstance, you should say your prayers with your child every night! Without being legalistic about it, never let a night go by when you do not pray with your children, if at all possible. This creates a positive habit in them and also teaches them the importance of prayer.

Sometimes I come into one of my children's room late, when my child is already in bed. I will discover him lying there with his eyes closed. He says, "Daddy, I'm already saying my prayers." I sit quietly on the side of the bed until he is finished. This is exactly the attitude we are looking to cultivate. We want them to say their prayers without us. We want prayer to be something they just do. We want it to be something they miss if they do not do it. For this reason be sure to make the practice of prayer consistent. One way you can model faith and build faith in your child is to pray with your child *every night!*

Being regular and consistent in prayer is one way to fulfill the biblical command to "pray without ceasing" (*I Thessalonians* 5:17). This instruction does not mean that we must be constantly uttering silent prayers to God throughout the day. Most of us find that

192

impossible to do. There is another way to look at this instruction, however. To pray without ceasing means simply to keep at it, always come back to it, never quit praying in both good and bad circumstances, and pray as often as we can throughout the day.

People have sometimes wondered if they can become *too prayerful*? Is there a line we can cross that gets us out of balance in life? How do you keep from getting "so heavenly minded that you are no earthly good," as the old saying goes? You may have known someone who was this way and you don't want your child headed in this direction. How do you keep their feet on the ground when teaching them about God and about prayer?

The answer is simply to keep them and their prayers engaged in their real life concerns. For most people, as long as they do not withdraw from their life and friends, their prayers do not get off balance. Keep your child's focus on practical things and the rest will work itself out. Sometimes people try to rush into a life of deep faith. They try to go from being a spiritual novice to a spiritual giant in a very short time. This generally does not work. The life of faith is like growing a giant oak tree – you cannot rush it. In fact if you give the seedling too much fertilizer you will scorch it. If you water it too much, you will drown it. A seedling needs a balance of the right things in the right proportions to grow into a healthy plant. Even at that, an oak grows slowly. This is the same with a child's spiritual life and yours. Do not rush it. Let it evolve. Let it grow. Teach your child in little increments. Give them a few pieces at a time, let them develop at their own pace, and watch their life of faith gradually but steadily grow.

There will come a point in your child's life when you are not there to make them pray. They will eventually go to college or move out. They will live on their own. They will have to make prayer a part of their routine, without you there to pray with them. Your hope is that by that time, they have come to experience the joy of quiet moments with God. Your hope that by then they will recognize the inner strength and peace that time with God gives them. If they do, they will find time to pray. They will keep their commitment to God and to prayer because they will realize that nothing else will center their lives like being in relationship with the living God. Nothing else but a real relationship with God will truly nurture their heart, soul, and spirit.

12

CONNECT YOUR CHILD TO THE CHURCH AND OTHER SPIRITUAL DISCIPLINES

TEACH YOUR CHILD TO WORSHIP

ONE NIGHT I HAD FINISHED PRAYING with one of my children. I leaned over and gave him a hug. I said something like, "I love you more than, ice cream and chocolate." I was trying to add a little fun to my expression of love. My son looked back and said, "I love you too Daddy." Then, he thought for a moment and said, "But I don't love you more than God." I was surprised by this response but pleased. I might have been offended but I was not because he had stated the correct priorities. I replied, "That's right. We always love God most of all." I knew at this moment that my son was grasping something very important. It is the simple but profound principle that if God comes first, everything else falls into place; if other things take first place, nothing is in the right order. When I approved his comment that evening, I helped affirm something he was coming to believe as true. God comes first. When we put God first, other things can then find their proper place and role. My son was also doing more than just restating a principle I had taught him. That God came first was something God was impressing on his heart through the gentle but powerful presence of the Holy Spirit.

The process of teaching your child to pray will help them align their lives with God. Why is this? Because in this process, over the years you pray with them, you will have the opportunity to teach them about God, answer their questions, model faith for them, and impart spiritual wisdom to them. As you talk to your child and pray with them over the years, you will gradually but steadily give them a Christian worldview, a mental picture of God, and some basic understandings about the Christian faith. In the process of teaching them to pray, you are also imparting to them essential knowledge about God. The Holy Spirit, whom the Bible calls the Spirit of Truth, will also give them spiritual insights that affirm the lessons you teach them.

Parents often underestimate the importance of their role in imparting the faith to their children. As a child, my parents told me that there was a God who loved me and who always watched over me. Did I need them to tell me this? Yes, because this was not something I would have known otherwise. They taught me some basic lessons about God and I believed them. I believed them

196

because it was my parents teaching me and I thought, at that point, they knew everything. Of course, they were telling me the truth. They were right that there is a God and that he loves me. That I came to understand God as a good God who watched over me, gave me a security for my life that I otherwise would not have had.

For this reason, parents should not underestimate the importance of little lessons, particularly in the early years. Tell your children about God. Affirm his existence. Tell them God loves them. Your children will believe you and it will implant these important principles in their hearts. The Holy Spirit will use these lessons to build faith in your child. In this final chapter, we talk about some further things you can do with your child to help them grow in their experience of God. At the heart of this is connecting them to the Christian church.

TEACH THEM TO WORSHIP

In this series we have focused on private prayer. That is, you have been teaching your child to have an individual and personal time of prayer, and making prayer a natural part of their lives. But there is another kind of prayer experience; it is the experience of corporate prayer, prayer with others. This may be prayer with several other people in some type of small group setting or it may be the experience of prayer in a worship service on Sunday morning. When you take your family to church, there are prayers in the

197

worship service; you need to help your child understand these and know how to connect with them.

Interestingly, while the focus of what you have been doing with your child has been helping them personally connect with God, you have also, without really trying, given them a first experience of praying with another person, because they have been praying, out loud, with you. As they get older, they may have opportunities to pray with other people, in youth group at church, or in some other setting, and you have helped your child gain a comfort level with doing so.

Let's think for a moment about the experience of corporate worship. At your church, there may be a time for study and learning, either Sunday School or a small group time, but then there is a time that is generally called worship or the worship service. During this time, the Bible is read and a sermon is preached. The sacraments may be celebrated on occasion. We join together with other people and lift our hearts to God with music and in song.

The term Christianity uses for this experience is "worship." One might ask when, exactly, the worship takes place? What is the essence and heart of a worship service? Sometimes, at the end of the worship service, you know that you have been to worship, but if someone were to ask you exactly when you worshipped, you might not be able to tell them. The whole event was the experience of the worship of God. At other times, you might be able to point to a particular moment. You might say, "I felt myself touched by something in one of the prayers." Or, "During Communion, I had a time of reflection in prayer." Or, "One of the songs we sang enabled

198

me to voice a prayer to God." Many churches have contemporary worship services. Contemporary worship music, at least some of it, is designed to help people worship in the moment. That is, it is designed so that you can make the words of the song your prayer and pray through the music as it is sung.

What you want to do is help your child appreciate and value the experience of worshipping God with other people. Think about this for a moment. The tendency is for kids to sit in worship and be bored. That's understandable; sometimes adults sit in worship and are bored. So how do we help engage our child with a corporate worship experience? One thing is to take them regularly. Take them to worship. Help them get used to being there. Make it a habit. Be engaged yourself; this sets an example for them to follow and gives them a positive view of the church. It is good for them to have warm experiences in church with their family and friends. In addition, it is important for you, as their parent, to provide a positive example. If you are regular in church, they will understand its importance. If you are always criticizing the sermon or the music or some other aspect of the experience, it will be hard to tell them to be positive. If you are positive about going to church, they will follow suit.

One thing to help them understand is that they have a responsibility in worship. It isn't really the preacher's job to entertain them. It's not the church's job to make things exciting, even though most churches try to do so. Instead, it is our job to come to worship in a good frame of mind, ready to bring ourselves to God in worship, irrespective of whether the preacher has a good sermon that day, or one that didn't quite hit the mark. As someone who preaches every week, I know that some days are just better than others, for the preacher, just like everyone else.

In spite of that, there is almost always something in the worship service with which you can connect and from which you can get something. If it isn't the sermon, it might be the music. People will sometimes say, "The sermon was not very good, but the music saved it for me." As a pastor, I have always wondered why people don't say, "The music was awful, but the sermon saved it for me." Oh well! If you come ready to worship, there will always be *something* God has for you. If nothing else, you can always *give* God your praise, gratitude, and prayers. Nothing will hinder you from doing that. To come ready for worship may be something as simple as getting a good night's sleep the night before.

There are a number of different styles of worship. My congregation has both a contemporary and a traditional style worship service. Since my children are preacher's kids, they grew up going to both and were required to like both. At least they were required to sit still and pay attention at both. When they got older, I would sometimes say to them, before the contemporary service: "Try to find some phrase, or sentence, or thought in the music that resonates with you, and make it into a prayer. Use the music to pray to God in your heart." I waited until they got into elementary school to do this, about the fourth grade. At that point, they were old enough to try to connect with God themselves during the worship experience.

There are also many moments in a traditional worship service in which your child can connect with God. For one thing, once they are old enough, you can expect them to listen and pay attention. Pay attention to the sermon. After about the fourth grade they ought to be able to listen and get something from the sermon. Your church may have a children's sermon and if so, they can be expected to be attentive, listen, and remember what was taught. You might revisit the children's sermon or the children's church lesson at lunch as a way to imprint the lesson in your child's mind.

There will certainly be prayers in the worship service. You can expect your child to be still and quiet. While listening to the pastor's prayer may not be the most stimulating experience for a child, you can instruct them to sit still and be in the presence of God. The Bible says, "Be still and know that I am God." Simply sitting quietly in prayer is a nurturing experience that your child ought to be able to do at some point. Additionally, the act of stewardship is an important part of worship. If your church has pledges, have your child make a pledge, then follow through with it. The goal is to help your child engage in the overall experience of worship and there are many ways they can do so.

One of the goals of your parenting is to help your child have good experiences in church. You want them to have friends at church, enjoy the classes and groups, and build relationships both with people their age and adults. We always wanted our children to feel affirmed and valued at church. When they are adults, and they think about places they have felt esteemed in their life, we want the church to be one of the places that comes to mind.

PRAYING FOR YOUR CHILD DAILY

As we said in a previous chapter, it is a primary responsibility of every parent to pray for their children. Your child needs someone to pray for them regularly. You, as their parent, are the person to whom God has primarily given this responsibility. For that reason, I want to give you a simple method for doing so.

One way to remember to pray for your child, every day, is include this as part of your evening prayers with your child. We did this with our sons in a simple way. Each night, I would pray for our family, mentioning every person by name. I started with myself and my wife, then included our children. Then I included extended family. For us, my prayer sounded something like this: "Please bless mommy and daddy (us), Robert and John (our sons), Grandmother and Papa (my parents), Gaga (my wife's mother), Aunt Vicki and Uncle Andrew (my sister and her husband), and Anna and Phillip (their children)." I said this as part of my prayer every evening. It became a simple way of remembering to pray for our family, including our children, every night. So every night, at some point in my prayers, I would say, "And bless Mommy and Daddy, Robert and John, Grandmother and Papa, Gaga, Aunt Vicki and Uncle Andrew, and Anna and Phillip."

I will occasionally also say an extended prayer for someone in the family, if they have a particular need. On occasion I will say a more detailed prayer for the child with whom I am praying. I might say, "And give Robert a good night's sleep. Help him to do well on his math test tomorrow and make good friends at school. And help his cold to get better." I make this just one part of the prayer I am praying; I make it natural and just include it my prayers.

If you have ever had someone pray a prayer specifically for you, you know what a meaningful experience this can be. This is true for your child as well. To pray for them specifically is a very special way you can nurture their spirit. They sense your love for them and, as we have said throughout, God hears our prayers. It matters that we pray for our children because God responds to our prayers.

In summary, be sure to make praying for your child a part of your regular prayers. Your child needs it and it is your responsibility as a parent. One way to do this is to pray for your family, by name, every night. On occasion, take some moments and specifically ask God to bless your child in some way particular to their life and needs, that touches things they care about, and that brings God into the real world where they live.

PRAYERS OF THE HEART

We have already talked about teaching our children to close their prayers with some simple phrases, such as, "Dear God, I love you very much." I want to say more about this kind of prayer in general and how you can use this type of prayer in guiding your children. There are many forms and types of prayers. Some prayers are full of praise and thanksgiving; others are filled with pain and anguish. At times people have used sections of scripture as a source for meditation, then made the ideas and words of scripture the substance of their prayers. There are many different ways to pray and all of them are useful. There is a kind of prayer that author Richard Foster, calls a "Prayer of the Heart." It is a simple prayer that people pray over and over until it becomes part of their thinking and feeling.

Our family has used the idea of "Prayers of the Heart" to implant important ideas into the hearts of our children. To move spiritual values from our child's head to their heart is an important practice. The world is going to fill our children's minds with many values. Not all those will be the values of God's kingdom. Some will tend to move our child's mind and heart away from God toward the values of the world. That is why it important for us to implant moral principles and values into the hearts and minds of our children. When we do so, we plant right and true values into the soil of their spirits and hearts.

We began with the simple phrase, "Dear God, I love you very much." As I have previously said, when we began this practice, I told our children that we were going to close our prayers every night with the phrase, "Dear God, I love you very much." This became the way we closed our prayers every evening and over a period of just weeks, it became a meaningful part of our prayers. The more we used this phrase, the more we prayed it with feeling. This was true for our children as well as myself. When they said it, they felt it and meant it. What better attitude of heart could they have than to know that God loves them and to affirm their love for God in return? What better life lesson would we want to teach our children from an early age than to nurture a real and expressed love for God? What better lesson in prayer could we give our child than to help them turn their heart toward the love of God?

To repeat what I said earlier in the book, I came to realize that this simple expression of love toward God was entering their hearts. As they said it, they began to believe it. They *did* love God and as they began to believe it, they began to *feel* it. They felt love for God. As I said before, this turns out to be an ancient principle of the spiritual life. Spiritual truths begin on the lips, then enter the mind, then finally are embraced by the heart.

I do not know for certain, but my hope is that this simple phrase will stay with our children. When they become adults and they say their prayers, I hope they will still close them with, "Dear God, I love you very much." If their lifestyle contradicts this statement, their prayer will call them to task and help keep them on the right path. When they get married and have children, I hope they will teach it to their children, and thus develop a new generation of people who truly love God not just in their heads, but with all their heart.

There are some other phrases our family has made into prayers from the heart. One is, "Forgive me my sins." We made this second phrase a part of how we close our prayers. In our family, we began to close our prayers with, "Dear God, forgive me my sins; I love you very much."

There are other prayers of the heart you might teach your child. One is, "Fill me with your Spirit." This is a way of reminding them that God's Spirit is present to give them strength and help. It also is an appropriate prayer, since the Bible encourages us to "be filled with the Spirit" (*Ephesians* 5:18).

Finally, we used the phrase, "Jesus, live in my heart every day." This was a way of teaching them that Christ not only lives in heaven, but in our hearts. Christ promises to enter the hearts and lives of all who ask him. *Revelation* 3:20 says, "Behold I stand at the door and knock. If anyone hears my voice and opens the door, I will come in to him and eat with him and he with me." If we want Christ to enter the hearts and lives of our children, why not have them ask him to do so? I cannot imagine that Jesus will not hear this prayer and answer, entering the lives of his little ones who sincerely ask him to do so. Our experience is that this is just what has happened to our children.

We began with one of these prayers of the heart then added to it. You may wish to rotate them through your times of prayer. Say one for a while then replace it with a new one. But once they get used to saying them, the phrases will simply become part of how they close their prayers. You are not only implanting moral principles into their heart, you are guiding their prayers around core spiritual principles. We ended up with four phrases we used to end our prayers. Our phrase was, "Forgive me my sins. Fill me with your Spirit. Jesus, live in my heart everyday. Dear God, I love you very much. Amen." In using these phrases, I felt like we helped them come to know God better as Father ("Dear God, I love you very much"), Son ("Jesus, live in my heart every day"), and Holy

Spirit ("Fill me with your Spirit"). We also helped them learn to live humbly before God ("Forgive me my sins").

CONCLUSION

THE CHRISTIAN HOUSEHOLD

The reality is that Christianity in America has all but lost the idea that the Christian faith is something that ought to be taught in the family. Two hundred years ago, this was understood in the United States. Fathers, in particular, understood that their responsibility was to train their children in the Bible and right living. This not only meant disciplining them into right behaviors but taking them to church and instructing them in the faith. In some religious traditions this meant learning catechism questions and answers on Sunday afternoons, along with memorizing psalms, and participating in family prayers. This was before there were so many distractions on Sunday afternoons, such as football games, movies to watch, and people to go see. In the era before the automobile, it was easier to stay home and be content with simple activities on Sundays because there were not many options. Today's distractions have made Sundays just like any other day, except for morning worship attendance.

I suggest however, that the idea of a Christian household should be rediscovered by American Christians. The home is the first and best place for the faith to be taught and passed along to children. It provides the perfect environment for children to learn about God in a safe, nurturing environment. For this to happen, however, you, as the parent, must build this into the structure of your family life.

One obvious thing you can do, if you are married, is love your spouse. Marriage can be difficult and tensions easily rise. When we are dating, we are each other's biggest fans. In marriage, however, there is the temptation to become each other's biggest critic. We see each other's faults in all their glory and what attracts us to someone when dating, irritates us in marriage. For these reasons, if we are not careful, our life with our spouse can be snippy, irritable, and confrontational. Children see this and pick up on it. When their parents do not get along, it creates anxiety in the lives of those whose world depends on the stability of their family. For this reason, do your very best to have a happy and peaceful relation with your spouse. Don't make a big deal of little faults and learn to love your spouse for his or her strengths. Remember also that marriage is "God's school for character." God is molding and refining you through it. He is helping you become kinder, more loving, and more patient. Stay in God's school and grow in his grace. God is able to help you create a deep and loving relationship with your spouse that will enrich your life, bring you joy, and be a stable foundation in which your children can grow into healthy young Christian disciples.

It is also important to understand the great opportunity you have, as a parent, to turn your child's life toward God. If you will teach your children about God, tell them simple truths about God, and nurture their spirits into faith, it will bear a rich reward. You will implant the seeds of faith in your child's life in a way that will allow them to grow into a Christian disciple, full of faith, good works, peace, and love. You will be able to effectively pass the Christian faith along to your child.

THE IMPACT OF PRAYER

We have made the case, in this book, that teaching your child to pray is the most effective way for you, as a parent, to pass the Christian faith along to your child. We have also asserted that doing so will change your child's life forever. Does teaching your child to pray really change their life? The answer is, "Yes." It changes their life because it brings them into an authentic relationship with God. How do you know this? Because you will watch it happen before your eyes. You will observe their relationship with God as it begins and grows. Like watching plants in your garden grow over time, you will be able to see their awareness of God and their understanding of him grow over the weeks, months, and years that they consistently, regularly, and faithfully pray.

What are you seeing? Not just the development of a set of skills. Not just a good habit they acquire. You are seeing them come to know God. They are coming to faith in Jesus Christ and God promises his Holy Spirit to all who place their trust in Jesus. In addition, Jesus promised to be with us when even two or three are gathered in his name. When you pray with your child, Christ is there with you. You sense this and your child will too. What you will observe is that God's Holy Spirit will descend into their life. You will watch as Christ indwells their life and becomes a living presence to them. You will see the transformation of their hearts by the cleansing and renewing work of God's presence. In short, you are seeing them come into the relationship with God that will save their lives, both in this world and the life to come. The good news is that this does not all depend on you. In fact, while you will lead them in this process, it is really the work of God in your child's life. The great thing, however, is that God is using you as the vehicle through which he will do his work.

Is this endeavor worth the effort? Yes. It is worth any effort it may take. It is worth overcoming any anxiety you may feel about your own life of prayer or your inability to teach your child about prayer. This is an endeavor that has eternal consequences and an everlasting reward. You are saving your child's life, though it is God who does it, not you. You are just the instrument whom God chooses to use in doing so. You are the one, however, who gets the joy of being used by God for the salvation of your child's heart, life, soul, and spirit. There is no greater joy any parent can have. There is no greater role any parent can play.

As I said at the beginning, we try to give our children all the advantages in life we can. We take them to piano lessons and little league practice. We make sure they do their homework so they will

212

maximize their abilities. We try to give them all the skills they need to be successful in life. How foolish it would be to give them everything else but neglect to lead them into a vital, authentic relationship with God. This is exactly what we give them, however, if we teach them to pray.

FOR PARENTS OF GROWN CHILDREN

I want to say something to parents of grown children, especially those who do not feel like they passed the Christian faith to their children as well as they wish they had. Perhaps you are one of those parents whose children now don't darken the doors of the church. Is there any hope? I believe there is.

There are some things you can do. The first is that you can pray regularly for you child. I have encouraged parents to pray daily for their children, and this is still your responsibility as a parent, no matter how old your children are. Pray for them. Pray for their salvation and that God will awaken their hearts to faith in him. The truth is that you have planted seeds of faith in their heart and life. If you took them to church when they were young, they had many opportunities to hear the gospel. Though it may not seem like those lessons made an impact, they may have made more than you think. Those seeds may be lying dormant in the soil of their life, waiting for the right moment to come to life or back to life. Pray that God will awaken faith in them and help them find their way back to him.

It may be that they have not lost their faith but are only averse, for whatever reason, to going to church.

Sometimes it takes a crisis or difficulty to turn people back to faith. No one wants their child to endure difficulties but life brings them to us all. It may be that God will use circumstances in their life to awaken in your child the faith that was implanted long ago. Pray that God will do so through whatever means he chooses.

The great historical example of the effectiveness of a parent's prayers is Monica, the mother of the 5th century theologian, Augustine. Monica prayed fervently, with many tears, for the conversion of her son, Augustine, who was an avowed pagan. At one point, she went to the Christian bishop, Ambrose, who was serving the church in her town of Milan. She begged him to speak to Augustine about turning his life to God. Ambrose did not feel it the right time to do so but was touched by her fervent prayers and many tears. He said to her, as a word of comfort, that it was not possible that a child who was the subject of so many prayers and tears should perish. His words were prophetic because Augustine would become a Christian and not only a Christian, but one of the greatest theologians of all time.

Pray for you child and, when you get the opportunity, like Monica, encourage them toward faith. This is what Monica did; she pleaded with her son to turn toward God. Though he refused to do so for many years, the words of his mother had an impact and were part of what God used to awaken his conscience. Grown children still care what their parents think of them and still want their approval, even when sin's influence makes it hard for them to see

214

the truth of God's love. Be wise and encourage faith in your grown child when you have opportunity, knowing that it may take time for your words and prayers to bear fruit. Author Abdu Murray tells how it took nine years of exploring religions and hearing about Jesus Christ before he opened his heart to God.[iv] That is not an uncommon story. It often takes many exposures to the gospel for it to take hold. When the time is right, God is able to open people's hearts to receive him. This is why we should never give up on others, especially our children, even when they seem resistant to the things of God.

There is an additional thing you can do as a parent of a grown child. You can implement these principles and practices with your grandchildren. You may not have taught your child to pray but you can teach your *grandchild* to pray. If your children are not doing this, it is especially important for you, as their grandparent, to do so. Use the occasions when your grandchildren spend the night with you to teach them to pray. Sit beside the bed and pray with them. Teach them to say thank you to God and ask God for what they need. They will respond with open hearts and with simple faith. You may have the opportunity to introduce your grandchildren to the living God by teaching them to turn their heart to God in prayer. *You* may be the person God will use for the salvation of your grandchild's life. This might also be an avenue for your grown child to be touched by God and renew their faith in him as well.

ONE MORE THING

What is left to do? Is there anything else? There is. There is another piece of the puzzle about which we have not talked, actually two pieces. If our child is to truly understand God and what God wants from them, they are going to have to understand the Bible. You have been guiding them in basic principles so far. You have been translating the Bible's themes and ideas into things they can understand. But they need to eventually come in contact with the Bible itself in a more substantial way. They need to understand the contents of the Bible and know how to use it to guide their life. This includes both the Old Testament and the New Testament. How can you do this?

This is a topic that is too long for this book but there is a way to introduce your child to the Bible over the years they spend, under your roof that will help them come to understand it. I have put this is another book titled, *Help Your Child Know, Understand, and Love the Bible.* This is an important piece of your child's Christian education. It is a vital piece because the Bible is how we know who God is. Without knowing the Bible, we do not have the understanding we need to fully follow God. We may have a picture of God but it may not be a true picture, or only partially true. If we want to truly understand God, we must listen to what God has told us about himself and how he expects us to live. The place we find all this is in the Bible.

In the early years of teaching your child to pray, you will give your child a general picture of God. Hopefully they will learn about God through the church you attend, which is why it is important for you to take them to church. They will learn about God through the questions they ask and the answers you give them. This is sufficient for a start. But at some point, they will need more.

In the early years, you are like a mother bird feeding her babies. She finds the food, chews it up, then gives it back to them in a digestible form. This is what you do with your child in their early years. You give them pieces and tidbits of information about God and life in forms they can digest. For example, you do not read them the entire four chapters in *Genesis* about Noah and the Ark. You summarize the story for them. That is fine in the beginning, but not sufficient for a fully mature Christian life. This is why, at some point, you have to get them reading the Bible on their own. In *Help Your Child Know, Understand, and Love the Bible,* we will look together at how to help your child do this, in a way that is fun and effective.

The other thing your child needs is to understand the Christian faith in a comprehensive way. The study of Christian belief is called *Christian theology.* The word "theology" literally means conversation about God. The Bible contains many kinds of literature, such as history, law, poetry, proverbs, and prophetic writings. Because the Bible contains so many different types of literature, our understanding of God and ourselves, must come from a broad study of the entire biblical story. It is the work of Christian theology to systematize what the Bible says and organize Christian

217

belief in understandable ways. In addition to introducing your child to the Bible, you need to teach them the beliefs of Christianity.

This includes understanding things such as, who is God, what has God done, what is the Trinity, how is God present in the world, who is Jesus Christ, what did Jesus do, how are we saved, how do we know right from wrong, etc. There are many questions such as these that need clear answers. It is the study of Christian belief that enables us to know the answers to these questions. The better we understand our faith, the better we can practice it and the more we can appreciate it.

One classic way to teach the faith to children is through the uses of catechisms. A catechism is a question and answer tool that takes you through a summary of Christian beliefs. Through the centuries, parents and church leaders have used catechisms to teach children, reading questions to them and explaining the answers. This is a simple way you can give your child an overview of Christian belief.

There is a wonderful catechism that is designed for this purpose. It is called *The Christian Catechism for Parents and Disciples*. It is designed for parents to use with their children. It consists of 52 sections, one for every Sunday of the year. Each section contains 4 or 5 questions and answers. Once a week or every so often, you can sit with your child and discuss these questions and answers. This catechism will give them clarity about Christian belief. It will introduce them to important Christian vocabulary words, such as incarnation, Trinity, Holy Spirit, atonement, justification, and more. Using it will also help you, as a parent, understand Christian belief better. To aid you in using this catechism, there is a parent's guide that explains the various questions and answers. The guide also provides discussion questions and scripture readings to use with your child. There is also a small booklet that contains the catechism itself. You will need a booklet for yourself and one for each of your children. This will become their booklet that teaches them about Christianity. It will hopefully be one they will keep and be able to refer to for many years. The parent's guide will help you as you go through the catechism with your child.

Thank you for your courage to embark on this process. You will do great and this will be much easier than you think. In fact, it will be one of the most rewarding experiences of your life. In teaching your child to pray, you are passing the Christian faith along to them. In doing this, you are being the parent your child needs you to be. You are giving them something that has eternal consequences. They will not recognize at this point what you have done but they will later. They will be *eternally* grateful and you will one day be able to celebrate God's goodness with them, in the kingdom of heaven, forever.

Visit us at www.creativechristianparenting.com, for more resources to help you, as a parent grow in your faith and pass your faith to your children. May God bless you! May God bless your family and make it into a very special place of God's presence and grace. Please allow me to pray with you and for you as we close this study.

"Dear God, what a privilege it is to be a parent; more than that, what a privilege to be a Christian parent. You have given me the great responsibility of guiding my child into the right path and particularly into the way of faith. Please help me as I nurture this special life you have put into my care. Send your Holy Spirit into my child's life. Touch them with your grace. Call them into some work, calling, vocation, or place of your choosing. Watch over all they do and keep them in the palm of your hand. O God I commit myself to be the parent you have called me to be. Give me wisdom and grace for this great work. For every child in my care, Lord Jesus, come and make your home in their heart. Holy Spirit, fill them with your grace. Father, forgive their sins and help them to love you, to truly love you, with all their heart, mind, soul, and strength, very, very, very, very much and more every day of their lives. O God of all good things, thank you again for the coming of your kingdom, in my child's life, in our families, and in our world. I love you and pray all these things in the name of our Savior, Jesus Christ. Amen.

STUDY GUIDE

1

RECOGNIZE THE IMPORTANCE OF YOUR ROLE AS A PARENT

Discussion Questions

1. Talk about what your parents did, if anything, to help you learn and embrace the Christian faith. What did they do well? What do you wish they had done better?

2. Talk about your church experience growing up, if you had one. What was that like? What do you think you gained from it? If you did not grow up in church, share what that was like, if you are comfortable doing so.

3. Where did you learn the most about God growing up? Was it from your parents? In what way? Was it from church? In what way? Was it from other sources?

4. What things have you done, so far to teach your children, help them get to know God, and pass along your faith? What has been the most successful? Least successful?

Bible Study

Read Deuteronomy 6:6–7

1. What words do you think this passage is talking about that are to be taught to the children? Look at Deuteronomy, chapters 5 and 6 for possible answers.
2. With what attitude were parents to teach these things to their children? What might this mean for us?
3. What might it look like if someone were to fulfill this instruction today?
4. What makes you most anxious and nervous about the idea of teaching spiritual things to your child?

Read Ephesians 6:4

1. Paul writes this instruction specifically to fathers, though perhaps both parents were intended. What do you think fathers bring to the spiritual training of their children? Mothers?
2. What do you think Paul meant by not provoking your children to anger? Can you think of situations in which this might happen?
3. What do you think the training and instruction of the Lord means? Can you think of any ways to do this?
4. What makes you most anxious and nervous about the idea of teaching spiritual things to your child?

Homework

Tell your child or children this week that God loves them and is always watching over them to take care of them.

2

CAN CHILDREN LEARN SPIRITUAL THINGS?

Discussion Questions

1. Do you remember saying prayers when you were a child? Who taught you to pray? What do you remember about these early prayers?

2. Looking back, what was the significance of your childhood prayers on your spiritual life? If you did not pray, what was the result of that?

3. Particularly when they are young, your children believe what you tell them about God. How might you use this opportunity to teach them about God? How comfortable do you feel doing this?

Bible Study

Read Luke 2:41-52

1. What do you think Jesus was like as a little boy?
2. What kind of religious training do you think Mary and Joseph gave him?
3. Do you think that Jesus prayed as a young boy? Why or why not? What might his life of prayer have been like?
4. At age 12 Jesus gave evidence of having both understood and assimilated a number of biblical stories, truths, and ideas. Do

you think this is evidence that he reflected on what he was learning as a child? How do you think he came to this depth of understanding?

5. If Jesus was able to come to this level of understanding by age 12, do you think we underestimate what our children can learn and understand? What indications do you see in your children of their ability to understand spiritual things?

Read Matthew 21:12-17

1. This story comes from the first Palm Sunday. Do you think the children fully understood what they were saying when they said "Hosanna to the Son of David?" How do you think God looks at the prayers of children when they are made with only limited understanding?
2. When the children acclaimed, "Hosanna to the Son of David," do you consider this a prayer? What kind of prayer?
3. What does it say to us about the prayers of children that Jesus seems to have approved of what these children were doing?
4. Have you done anything up to this point to teach your children to pray? What have you done? What seems to have been successful? What has not been successful?

Homework

Do some things to nurture the spiritual dimension of your child's life this week, such as reading the Bible to them, saying a prayer with them, telling them something about God, telling them why you believe in God, hugging them and telling them that you love them and God loves them too, etc.

3

UNDERSTAND THE NATURE AND PRACTICE OF PRAYER, PART 1

Discussion Questions

1. What do you think is the most difficult thing about prayer?

2. Do you have a time or place in which you find it easiest to pray?

3. How do you feel about the statement that "God answers prayers?" In what form do you think these answers usually come?

4. Do you feel like you have gotten "better" at praying over the years?

5. Do you typically read the Bible when you pray? Why or why not?

6. What is most difficult for you about reading the Bible?

Bible Study

Read Matthew 7:7-11

1. The invitation, ask, knock, and seek, is repeated three times for emphasis. Given such an invitation, why do you think people find being consistent in prayer so difficult?

2. Jesus teaches about the generosity and willingness of God in these verses. Do you experience God as willing and generous when you pray or do you experience God differently?

3. To what kind of "good things" (verse 11) might Jesus have been referring?

4. Luke's version of these statements by Jesus (Luke 11:9-13) says that Jesus will give the "Holy Spirit" to those who ask him. What do you think is the difference between the Holy Spirit and "good things?"

Read Matthew 6:9-13

1. The Lord's Prayer is generally broken down into 6 petitions (or requests). How would break the prayer down into its various different petitions?

2. The prayer starts with focusing on God, thanking God, and asking for coming of God's kingdom. If God's kingdom were to come, in what ways would you benefit? Do you typically start your prayers with some type of thanksgiving?

3. Why do you think Jesus wanted people to pray for the coming of God's kingdom? What specific impact in this regard do you think our prayers have? Will our prayers make a difference in this regard (or only our actions)?

4. How important do you think it is to include these prayers for ourselves in our regular prayers: for daily bread, for

forgiveness, for help with temptation? How often are these part of your regular prayers?

Homework

Consider your own life of prayer? How would you rate yourself in your exercise of this Christian discipline? What needs improvement? See if you can do one thing better this week.

4

UNDERSTAND THE NATURE AND PRACTICE OF PRAYER, PART 2

Discussion Questions

1. What about your morning routine is either conducive to prayer or *not* conducive? Your evening routine?

2. Do you typically take time during the day to stop and consciously say a prayer? What occasions prompt this?

3. Do you typically combine the practice of reading the Bible with prayer? If so, what benefits do you find from doing so? If not, why not?

4. How good do you think you are at listening to God in prayer? What are ways that you have learned to hear God's "voice?"

5. How do you "sense God's presence" when you pray? How would you describe this to someone else?

6. Why do you think the author says that we should not focus on our feelings when we pray?

7. What do you feel like you have learned over the years about prayer that has been helpful?

Bible Study

Read Jeremiah 33:2-3

1. The phrase, "Call to me," is an invitation to prayer. It may also be seen as a "commandment" to prayer. In what ways are we commanded to pray? Are we being disobedient when we do not pray? Why do you think prayer is so important for the Christian?
2. How do you think God typically answers prayers? Do you think that God more often grants objective answers or are they usually more internal and subjective ones? That is, does God more often change circumstances or does God change us?
3. God says to Jeremiah that he will show him "hidden things." What things would you like to know or understand that God might be able to reveal?
4. Do you tend to feel like more of your prayers are answered or go unanswered? Why do you think some prayers seem to go unanswered?

Read Philippians 4:6-7

1. What things are you typically most anxious about? Could these be subjects for your prayers? Do you typically pray about them?
2. Do you feel like you can pray about everything? Are there certain things you feel like you should not pray for?
3. How comfortable do you feel about praying for yourself? On a scale of praying for yourself too little (1) to praying for yourself too much or exclusively (10), where would you rate yourself?
4. Do you typically feel a sense of peace after praying about something? Or do you tend to still be anxious?
5. Why do you think Paul includes thanksgiving in with prayers of petition? Why do you think Paul says that our requests should be "with thanksgiving?"

Homework

1. Continue to reflect on your own practice of prayer. Remember that Christian disciples have "disciplines." Continue to work to be consistent with some regular discipline of prayer.
2. Consider experimenting this week with a practice that the author suggested. In prayer say, "God, what do you want me to pray for?" Then pray about the things that come to your mind.

5

FINDING A TIME AND PLACE

Discussion Questions

1. What was your bedtime ritual when you were growing up? How has this influenced what you do with your child now?

2. Describe your family's morning routine, especially as it concerns your child or children. What works well in your routine? What does not work as well?

3. Describe your family's evening routine, especially the bedtime routine. What works well in this routine? What does not work well?

4. What would you have to do in your family to create a bedtime routine that would allow you to sit with your child and pray with them?

5. Does the idea of praying out loud with your child make you nervous? Why? Why not?

Bible Study

Read Deuteronomy 11:18-21

1. Why do you think bedtime might be a good time to pray with your child and teach your child to pray? What problems do you think this approach might present?

2. Why do you think God instructed parents to teach their children about God? What would you say to someone who said that we ought to not teach our children about God, so they can "make up their own minds?"

3. How do you think that teaching your child to pray might serve to teach them about God?

4. In addition to the evening, the passage mentions several times and places where you can talk to your child/children about God. Can you think of ways you might talk to your children about God, at home, when out, and in the morning?

5. How do you think learning to pray their own real prayers might help your child, as the passage says, take the words of God into their heart and soul?

Read Psalm 63:1-6

1. To what degree do you think children might be able to develop a relationship with God through prayer? Can they pray prayers of thanksgiving? Confession? Petition? What are your honest thoughts about this?

2. Do you find that bedtime, just before we fall asleep, is a particularly good time to pray? Why? Why not?

3. It seems that, for David in this psalm, prayer creates both a deep sense of satisfaction and also an ongoing hunger. Why do you think this is? Is this a common experience?

4. How do you think people typically develop a hunger for God? Is this something that can be developed and nurtured? How? What would you need to do to allow this to develop further in your own life?

5. When do you typically find time to think about God? For David, as a shepherd, it was the night watches. Are there times when you find yourself relaxed enough that your thoughts turn to God?

Homework

If you do not have a bedtime routine that involves putting your children to bed, begin to create one. If you are married, be sure that both father and mother participate, if possible. Try to create for your child a warm experience of being tucked in, kissed on the forehead, and affirmed, right before they go to sleep.

6

GET STARTED WITH YOUR CHILD

Discussion Questions

1. If you do not already have a time of prayer with your child, how easy or difficult does this process sound?

2. If you already have a process of praying with your child, what is working well? Not so well?

3. If you did not have a bedtime routine, were you able to create one after last week's lesson?

4. Do you find that your child tends to be grateful? Do you think saying prayers of thanksgiving at night might help create a more grateful attitude?

Bible Study

Read Luke 17:11-19

1. Do you think that our degree of gratitude influences our overall happiness in life? What is the relationship between prayers of gratitude and seeing the cup "half full" versus "half empty?"
2. Do you generally feel that you are sufficiently grateful to God for his blessings? What might you do to increase your sense of gratitude?
3. In this incident, it was the Samaritan who showed gratitude. Samaritans were social and religious outcasts to the Jewish people. What might there have been about the Samaritan's situation or attitude that made him more grateful than the others? What do you think makes for grateful children?
4. From God's point of view, what is the purpose of our prayers of gratitude? Are they for God's benefit or ours? How might more time spent in prayers of gratitude improve your life of prayer?

Read Ephesians 5:18-20

1. What do you think gratitude and music have to do with being filled with the Spirit? Why do you think Paul puts these things together? Explain.
2. Paul instructs people to "give thanks always and for everything." Are there things for which you find it hard to give thanks? What are they? Does Paul's instruction *not* apply to these things? Why or why not?
3. Paul's instruction to be filled with the Spirit is a "command," as if we have some control over it. Do you think we can intentionally be filled with the Spirit? What do we need to do? How much control over this do you think we have?

4. In what sense do you think being in church helps children "be filled with the Spirit?" Do you think being involved in church helps children sense God? How?
5. Have you found any good ways to connect your child to Christian music? How? What advantages do you see in Christian music, either hymns, worship songs, or contemporary Christian music?

Homework

This week, start the process of praying bedtime prayers with your child or children.

7

MAKING PRAYER A HABIT WITH YOUR CHILD

Discussion Questions

1. If you started the process of praying with your child this week, how did it go? What went smoothly? What were the challenges?

2. If you did not start the process, what held you back?

3. If you have already been praying with your child what have you changed if anything because of this study?

4. We discussed prayers of thanksgiving in the previous lesson. When you thank God for your blessings, do you tend to mention the same things every time? What are they? Do you think you should "branch out" in your thanksgivings? How might you do so?

5. Do you tend to pray for the same people and things? Do you think you should widen the scope of those people and things for which you pray? How might you do so?

6. Think of as many things as you can that your child might say "thank you" to God for. Is there a way you might use these to prompt and encourage your child in their prayers of thanksgiving and expand their thinking in this area?

Bible Study

Read the following passages from the book of *Proverbs*

Proverbs 13:24 - Whoever spares the rod hates his son, but he who loves him is diligent to discipline him.
Proverbs 22:6 - Train up a child in the way he should go; even when he is old he will not depart from it.
Proverbs 22:15 - Folly is bound up in the heart of a child, but the rod of discipline drives it far from him.
Proverbs 29:17 - Discipline your son, and he will give you rest; he will give delight to your heart.
Proverbs 23:13, 14 - Do not withhold discipline from a child; if you strike him with a rod, he will not die. If you strike him with the rod, you will save his soul from Sheol.

1. Child psychologist John Rosemond has said that if you say, "No" to your child about four times as often as you say, "Yes," you have the right balance.[v] What do you think about this statement?
2. What methods of discipline were used with you growing up? Do you tend to use those same methods or different ones?
3. What methods of discipline do you tend to use with your child or children? What seems to be the most effective? Least effective?
4. What is the most aggravating thing your child does? The most disappointing? What are you having the hardest time correcting?
5. How comfortable are you with corporeal punishment, i.e. spanking? If you use this type of discipline, what works well? What anxieties do you have about how you discipline your child or children?

Read Deuteronomy 8:5, 6 and Hebrews 12:5-13

1. In what ways does God discipline us? How do people actually experience God's discipline in their lives?

2. What do we learn about disciplining our child or children from God's exercise of discipline with us? Are we tougher than God or easier?

3. What do you think is the right balance between positive encouragement to do the right thing and negative consequences when our child does the wrong thing? Do your parenting instructions tend to be more positive or negative?

4. What do you think is the right balance between strict discipline and mercy? How well balanced is your parenting? In your own life, do you tend to experience God as too strict or too lenient? How should this inform your parenting?

Other discussion questions on discipline

1. It has been said that, "external discipline helps children develop internal discipline?" What do you think about this statement? Can you think of examples of how this has worked in your child's life?

2. It has been said that you should discipline your child strictly when they are young, so you can ease up when they become teens. If you do not discipline them early, they will not learn how to control their emotions and desires. When you try to discipline them as teens, you will not get compliance but rebellion. What do you think about this idea? How is this working in your family?

3. Do you feel like you have an effective method of discipline in your family? Why or why not? If not, how can you find a more effective method?

Homework

Think about the methods of discipline you use with your children. Consider any changes that need to be made and how you can implement them.

8

PRAYING WITH TEENAGERS AND OTHER CHALLENGES

Discussion Questions

1. From what you remember of your teenage years, how did your attitudes, needs, and perspectives change when you became a teen? How did your spiritual life change?

2. In what ways were you aware of your spiritual needs as a teenager?

3. What things were most helpful and impactful on your spiritual life as a teen? What things hindered your spiritual life?

4. Can you think of times when your child "wore you down" with their persistence? What did they want? Did you give in to them or not? Have you ever turned the tables and used this technique with your teen?

5. If you have a teenager, what do you observe about how this stage in life is impacting their spiritual life?

Bible Study

Read Luke 18:1-8

1. Do you think it is appropriate to be persistent in trying to nurture the life of your child, even when they become teenagers? What might this look like in your family?
2. Name as many ways as possible to nurture the spiritual life of your child. Think particularly about what might be affective for the various ages of your children.
3. Do you know anyone who seems to have nurtured the faith of their teenager or presently is nurturing it? What did they do or are they doing?
4. Do you know families in which the teens were not nurtured in their faith? What was not done and should have been done? What have been the results?
5. Jesus said that God would grant the widow "justice." Do you think God will help you if you truly, for godly purposes, want to nurture the life of your child? In what ways might he do so?

Read Daniel 1:3-6, 8-16

1. Daniel was a young man at this point, probably a teenager. How do you think Daniel might have developed such deep faith?
2. Can you think of other teenagers in the Bible who displayed faith?
3. Do you think we underestimate our teens in regard to their ability to believe in God, understand God, and follow God?

4. If you have a teenager, what have you done to nurture their life of faith? What else might you do?

5. What can you do to nurture the faith of other teens you know? Is there any teen in your sphere of influence that needs a second father or mother to nurture them? How might you be that person?

Homework

Consider adding the phrase "Forgive me my sins" to your nightly prayers with your child. If you have a teenager, either begin a time of prayer with them or continue to pray with them. Think about ways you can nurture the faith, understanding, and devotion of your teen.

9

QUESTIONS CHILDREN ASK

Discussion Questions

It is good to practice answering tough questions. See if you can develop short, simple, but biblically faithful answers to these questions a child might ask. Write down your answer. After you have come up with an answer, read the passages from the Bible. Revise your answer if necessary. Then share your answers.

1. Who is God?

    Verses to consider: Genesis 1:3-5, Deuteronomy 6:4-5, Exodus 34:5-7, I John 1:5

2. Where does God live?

    Verses to consider: Psalm 11:4, Isaiah 66:1, Psalm 103:19

3. What does God look like?

Verses to consider: John 1:18, I Timothy 1:17, I John 4:12, John 4:24

4. Who made God?

Verses to consider: Genesis 1:1-2, Revelation 1:8, Revelation 4:11

5. Does God love everyone?

Verses to consider: Psalm 86:5, John 3:16, I Timothy 2:4, I John 4:7-10

Homework

Think about questions your child has asked. Do you feel like you answered the question well? If not, look for an occasion to improve and refine your answer with your child.

10

MORE QUESTIONS AND ANSWERS

Discussion Questions

What are some "tough questions" your child has asked or you worry that they will ask.

Without reference to the chapter, write down an answer to these questions, then look up the scripture references. Make revisions to your answers after doing so if necessary. Share your answers with others. Then you might want to see how the author answered these questions.

Questions About Jesus

1. Who is Jesus?

    Verses to consider: Matthew 16:13-16; Colossians 1:16-17; Luke 1:32-33

2. Who is God, Jesus or God?

    Verses to consider: John 1:1-5; Philippians 2:5-11; Matthew 28:19

3.   When did God create Jesus?

Verses to consider: Micah 5:2; John 3:16; John 17:24

Questions About Heaven and Hell

1.   Am I going to heaven?

Verses to consider: John 3:16; Matthew 18:3-4; Mark 10:13-16;

2.   Am I going to hell? I sometimes do bad things.

Verses to consider: Mark 5:36; Acts 16:31; Romans 10:9

3.   Is my friend who does not believe in Jesus going to hell?

Verses to consider: I Timothy 2:3-4; Luke 14:23; Matthew 28:19-20

Questions About Church

1. If God is everywhere why is it important to go to church?

Verses to consider: Matthew 18:20; Acts 2:42; Colossians 3:16

2. Why is church sometimes boring?

Verses to consider: Acts 11:25-26; John 14:15; I Timothy 3:15

3. Why are there so many different denominations?

Verses to consider: I Corinthians 12:5; Romans 12:3; Acts 15:36-40

Homework

Should you get a tough question from your child this week, do your best to answer it. Trust your ability to be able to do so. Give a better or more refined answer the next night if you need to.

11

NEXT STEPS IN PRAYER WITH YOUR CHILD

Discussion Questions

Here are some ideas you might use to enhance your time of prayer with your child. Discuss them and decide if there are any you might use.

1. Create a prayer list on a 3 x 5 card and put it in your child's Bible. Pull it out once a week and pray for the people on the list.

2. Say a prayer in the car before you go on a vacation or otherwise long trip.

3. When you pass a wreck on the highway, tell everyone in the car to say a short prayer in their heart that everyone will be okay.

4. Go through the alphabet for prayers of thanksgiving. Start with "A." Each night do another letter. Try to think of things you are thankful for that begin with the letter of the night. Remember to say "thank you" to God for these things in your prayer that evening.

5. Be sure to touch your child when you pray, as seems appropriate. If you can place your hand on your child's leg, arm, or ankle while you pray for them, it gives them a physical sense of connection with you.

6. Pick a verse from the Bible to use in your prayers. Tell them the Bible verse every day for a week. Find various things in that verse to pray for every night. For example, you might choose, Galatians 5:22, 23 (the fruit of the Spirit). Focus on one fruit of the Spirit each night and pray that God will help you develop that characteristic. Passages you might use for this are: Romans 12:9-21, I Corinthians 13; Joshua 1:6-9, Exodus 20:1-17.

7. Think about when you can have a time of family prayer when everyone prays together. When could you do so and how might you organize it?

8. Be sure to say the blessing at meal times when you eat at home. Hold hands for the prayer.

9. Teach them to pray for 5 things using their hand. The thumb is to pray for their family. The next finger is to pray for their church. The next is to pray for their school teachers, friends, and activities. The next is to pray for someone else who has a need. The little finger is to pray for themselves. You might go through these, one finger at a time during a week.

10. One night ask them what they think they are good at. Tell them to thank God for those gifts. Another night ask them who is their favorite teacher. Have them thank God for that teacher and pray for them in their prayers that evening.

11. Teach your child the "Lord's Prayer." Explain it as you go through it. Say it enough that they will remember it. Come back to it every now and then to be sure your child continues to remember it.

Bible Study

Read the Luke 18:9-14

1. Why do you think the Tax Collector, who would otherwise not appear to have been very religious, went up to the temple to pray?
2. Was there anything wrong with the religious acts that were a part of the life of the Pharisee? Do you think the parable disparages those or only his attitude?
3. Which of these two people do you think you would rather have as a next door neighbor? Why?
4. What do you think Jesus meant when he said that the Tax Collector went home justified? What does it mean that the Pharisee did not?
5. What does Jesus mean when he says that everyone who exalts himself will be humbled and everyone who humbles himself will be exalted?

Other Discussion Questions

1. Share your ongoing experience of praying with your child. What have you done new and/or differently because of this study? What difference is it making?
2. How hard is it for you to be consistent in your prayers with your child? How successful are you in this area?
3. What do you think about the idea of praying for your child every day? Do you think this is an important parental responsibility? How might you be sure to do this every day?

Homework

This week, as part of your prayers with your child, pray for your child's particular needs. Think of some needs of your child and pray for them specifically, as part of your nightly prayers. Also thank God for their talents and abilities. Such a prayer might sound something like this: "Dear God, we pray that you will give Mary a good mind to learn at school this week. Thank you that you have made her smart. Thank that she loves soccer and is good at it. Help her this week to make good friends, do good in school, and be the best person she can be. Thank you that you love her and have made her very special. Bless us all and keep us in your care this week."

12

CONNECT YOUR CHILD TO THE CHURCH AND OTHER SPIRITUAL DISCIPLINES

Discussion Questions

1.   How has starting the process of praying with your child or children gone? If you have not started, what is holding you back? What problems are you encountering at this point?

2. For fathers, have you been participating in this process? If so, how has it gone? If not, what is holding you back? In general, do you think your child has also found this a good bonding time with you?

3. We have stressed the importance of being consistent in praying with your child. How consistent are you? If not, what needs to change?

4. We have stressed the importance of taking your family to church. Talk about how well you are doing having your children in church.

5. Has the structure of saying prayers of thanksgiving and prayers of petition become comfortable for you child? Do you ever hear them say things in their prayers that surprise you?

Bible Study

Read Revelation 5:6-14

1. This passage describes John's vision of heavenly worship. What things in this passage relate to worship?
2. Why do you think there are 24 elders around the throne of God? What might they represent?
3. Verse 8 says that the elders have harps and golden bowls full of incense, which represent the "prayers of the saints." What is important to you about this image?
4. Notice that the elders sing in heaven. In your experience, what is the importance of singing as a form of worship? What do you find meaningful in doing so? What is challenging?

5. Why do you think the songs in this passage focus on praise to God and the Lamb? What feelings might being in the presence of God elicit from people? From you?
6. What are some ways you can help connect your child to your church's service of worship?

Prayers of the Heart

Discuss how you might use some of these prayers of the heart with your child.

"Forgive me my sins."
"Jesus, live in my heart every day."
"Fill me with your Spirit."
"Dear God, I love you very much."

ADDITIONAL HELPS

Watch for the books:

Help Your Child Know, Understand, and Love the Bible

Teach The Christian Faith To Your Children
And Learn It Yourself By Using
The Christian Catechism For Families And Disciples

Visit www.creativechristianparenting.com for resources to nurture your faith and your family.

NOTES

[i] "Six Reasons Young Christians Leave Church." *Barna Group*, 27 Sept. 2011, www.barna.com/research/six-reasons-young-christians-leave-church/. Accessed May 14, 2020.

[ii] Pomerantz, Dorothy. "Super Model, Super Mogul." *Forbes*, 27 Feb. 2012.

[iii] Cathy, S. Truett. *Eat More Chikin: Inspire More People.* Looking Glass Books, 2002, page 92.

[iv] Malhotra, Ruth. "Abdu Murray on Islam and Christianity: Global Crises Present Christians With Unique Opportunities." *RZIM*, www.rzim.org/read/rzim-global/abdu-murray-on-islam-and-christianity-global-crises-present-christians-with-unique-opportunities.

[v] I heard him say this in a lecture held in Charlotte, North Carolina

Made in the USA
Columbia, SC
10 August 2021